Make Love

WHENEVER POSSIBLE WHEN

married with children

Make Love

WHENEVER POSSIBLE WHEN

married with children

CR

Leslie Kaplan
and
Peg Melnik

To order additional copies of this book, contact:
www.amazon.com

23771

Contents

The three universal truths of living with kids

CHAPTER 1
BE AN OPPORTUNIST
MAKE LOVE WHENEVER POSSIBLE

Peg's story
Leslie's story

Peg's story
Leslie's story

CHAPTER 2
DATE YOUR LOVER
DON'T PUT OFF DATING FOR TWO DECADES
UNTIL YOUR KIDS ARE CONVENIENTLY IN COLLEGE

CHAPTER 3
BE KIND TO YOUR LOVER
EVEN GROWN-UPS NEED TO BE NURTURED

CHAPTER 4
PLAN FOR CHAOS

CHAPTER 5
NEGOTIATIONS
MARRIAGE IS ONE LONG, UNWIELDY NEGOTIATION
KEEP CLOSING THE DEAL

CHAPTER 6
STAY CLOSE TO YOUR SPIRIT
FIND WAYS TO NURTURE YOURSELF

Acknowledgements

This book is a triumph. Anyone who's married with kids knows how hard it is to find time to take a shower much less write a book, so we have a lot of people to thank.

We deeply appreciate the patience, love and understanding of our husbands and children. We could not have accomplished this project without our public relation advisors Jenny Kaplan and Susan Barnes, our gifted photographer Christophe Genty, and amazing graphic designers, Session Creative and Gale Peck.

We would also thank our esteemed editors Laurie Dawson, Amy Scharch and Bruce Baird.

We dedicate this book to our spiritual mentor Daisaku Ikeda whose guidance continually revitalizes our spirit.

If you have feedback, we'd love to hear from you. Contact us at Makelovewheneverpossible.com or *melniknote@aol.com.*

We dedicate this book to our husbands and children, who unwittingly served as the raw material for this book. While it's a challenge to be married with kids, we couldn't imagine a life without them. Aside from making great copy, they are a delight.

Introduction

"Make Love Whenever Possible When Married With Children" is playful and poignant with spirited vignettes like "Seduce your spouse with humor," "Be a flasher," and "Experience the post-vasectomy sexual renaissance." Leslie Kaplan and Peg Melnik teamed up to write the book based on the following prescription program for staying sane within the madness of family life:

1. Be an opportunist. Make love whenever possible.
2. Date your spouse. Don't put off dating for two decades until your kids are conveniently in college.
3. Tend to your spouse. Even adults need to be nurtured.
4. Plan for chaos.
5. Become a top-flight negotiator. Marriage is one long, unwieldy negotiation. Keep closing the deal.
6. Keep close to your spirit. Find ways to nurture yourself.

The co-authors firmly believe couples are living their most challenging years when they have children under their roof. Parents inhabit a different world than do those without children, one ruled by the needs of small people. The sheer responsibility that comes with parenthood can, over time, complicate even the healthiest marriage.

While the divorce rate in America is at an astonishing 62 percent, staying happily married with children is not an insurmountable challenge as long as you realize it requires a kind of vigilance. It requires perspective, insight and, most importantly, the energy to keep a strong connection with your spouse.

The authors use wisdom and wit to detail valuable tips drawn from their own experiences—both positive and negative. The book is broken into six chapters, with a series of vignettes approximately one to three pages in length.

Some of the more visual scenes from the book include playing hooky with your spouse, renewing marriage vows at Notre Dame and absent-mindedly driving to work with a plateful of cookies flying off the roof of the car, littering the road.

Kaplan and Melnik's survival guide will no doubt be a compelling read, the best-selling bible for the married-with-kids crowd.

The three universal truths of living with kids

Kaplan and Melnik want to initiate you into what they call "The Family Orbit" by briefing you on the orbit's three universal truths:

1. Children jolt parents into warp drive. They have a whirlwind of frantic needs to be tended—food, clothing, shelter and comfort—to name a few.
2. Children spend most of their waking hours interrupting parents, so parents need to acclimate themselves to distraction. In fact, parents need to manage their time based on the notion that kids are, by nature, interrupters.
3. Children pull parents in more directions than imaginable with their activities—Girl Scouts, piano, soccer, swim team, play dates and parties. This harried pace makes it a challenge for parents to schedule time to nurture their significant other and keep their relationships rock solid.

Chapter 1

Be an opportunist

Make love whenever possible

☙

Steal time: Play hooky

Employers would not advocate what I am about to advise: Play hooky once in a while.

When you're both working and strapped for time alone, you may reach a point once or twice a year when you feel as though you're living with a stranger. If this happens when all of your babysitters are in the middle of final exams or prepping for prom night, there is only one thing left to do: Call in sick and send the kids off to school as usual. Steal time. Watch time stand still for a few hours.

The kids are out of the house. No one calls because everyone thinks you're at work. You actually have fresh energy because it's the beginning of the day and you're not sick. Why wait until you get a fever to be alone with your spouse? As my Jewish grandmother would say if she were alive today, "Who needs to know?"

We begin our day of hooky with a leisurely breakfast at a restaurant off the beaten path. Then we take a hike near a lake. We talk. We enjoy the crowdless park on this business day when we're at play.

My husband and I experience this stolen time at least once a year, and it's precious. Making love in the middle of the day when we're actually wide awake is truly a unique experience for those of us who are married with kids. It's almost surreal.

I got a 45-minute back rub at 1 p.m. and made love without rushing through the experience, without worrying about the kids hearing me moan. Afterward I lay in our bed and stared at the sun streaking in the window. I listened to Boccelli sing at me for 30 minutes straight. Luxurious.

I know it sounds wild. Well, it was.

Disclaimer: If you both work for the same company, steal time cautiously.

Love me tender

Sometimes make love with your husband in the bathroom when you're guests at a fancy dinner party.

Just for the suspense of it.

Just for the impracticality of it.

Just for the hilarity of it.

I know what you're thinking. What would Miss Manners say? How could such an unorthodox thing happen?

Well, as I recall, one of us made a pass and it was well received.

It was not comfortable sex. It was better than that. It was invigorating sex. It was a secret and spontaneous and ridiculous and sweet. And surprisingly, uninterrupted. If you plan to partake in this kind of unorthodox behavior, be sure the host has more than one bathroom and, for Lord's sake, be sure to lock the door.

I think making love in offbeat locations is a grand idea. I'm hoping someone will cut to the chase and write the book "The Best Places to Make Love" as a sequel to "The Best Places to Kiss."

One ideal offbeat location is a cornfield, believe it or not. We made love in one once, back when we lived in the Midwest . . . or as I say when we did time in the Midwest. The lovemaking was wild and passionate and risky. Luckily no farmer with a shotgun spied us.

Of course, now that we're married with kids, we have a house full of small-framed spies. That's why we have to resort to offbeat, well-secured locations from time to time.

I once gave my husband a card with Elvis playing guitar on the cover. Inside it said "Love me Tender," a coupon of sorts for sexual shenanigans any time, anywhere.

Experience the post-vasectomy sexual renaissance

Our post-vasectomy sexual renaissance proves one thing. When one does not have to worry about getting pregnant, one can have a lot of fun.

Once we decided not to have any more children, we didn't want to use contraceptives. We had used various forms of birth control for more than a decade and felt it was time for a change.

When my husband offered to have a vasectomy, I was surprised, elated and thrilled. My body has been through a war of sorts. My scars are in the form of stretch marks and a weak bladder. It was an act of kindness and commitment on his part to have the vasectomy. And it was much appreciated.

Little did I know how great our love life would be once this procedure was complete. We are now experiencing spontaneous, carefree, frequent and incredibly loving sex. It's as if we're young lovers. We feel as though we're 20, yet we're over 40, our careers are set, we have our 2.5 kids and a house with a picket fence that we're buying from the bank.

In the past we considered ourselves lucky to have sex once a week, but twice a month was average. It was sort of a crapshoot. One never knew. But now three or four times a week is not unusual. Chalk it up to chance? No way. It's the post-vasectomy sexual renaissance.

Harmonious and exciting lovemaking is crucial for any relationship. But when you're married with kids it's not only important, it's essential. Often good sex can mean the difference between simply being roommates who keep house and being lovers who actually look forward to being together.

I've noticed that throughout our marriage when the intimacy is there, when the sex is good and regular, all of the responsibilities of parenthood are bearable. But when we have not been intimate for two or three or four weeks we become grouchy, irritable, out-and-out nasty. Every small spill of juice on the carpet, every diaper change, every tussle between siblings drives us batty. We can become nasty to each other. "I didn't get any sleep last night because I was the one rocking the kid." Strangely, when the sex is good and frequent we're good sports when it comes to sleepless nights, messy diapers and crying babies.

Be a flasher

In the past few years I've taken up a risqué sport: flashing body parts. Of course I only flash my husband, and I'm a premeditated flasher. I am careful to strike only when my kids are out of sight.

Flashing has had an interesting affect on my husband. He retaliates and flashes back. I was surprised by the playfulness this has unleashed in our marriage, a sneaky way to be sexy with each other in the family orbit.

Before we took up flashing, we compartmentalized our marriage with sex set aside for the off hours, when the kids were down for the night. But these days, when the kids aren't looking, we can steal a little sex—a flash, a pinch, a lingering wet kiss. Of course sometimes a flashing is interpreted as a full-out pass. Once when the kids were at the neighbors, I flashed my husband and one thing led to another, postponing dinner. I think there is something to this flashing of body parts that triggers the sexual beast in all of us.

If you think it's not a good idea for mom and dad to let sexual feelings flow between them when children are wide awake and sometimes even in the next room, you're dead wrong. That twinge of sexuality creates intimacy, a good laugh and a lingering warmth that is good for children and other living things.

Once when my husband kept pecking my cheek, I struggled to get away and told my daughter to come rescue me, complaining that dad was loving me too much. She laughed a little as she came to my rescue. I saw that sheepish smile of hers and the blush beneath. I thought to myself, she gets a kick out of the fact that we're playful with each other. She picks up on the love between us.

Considering kids pick up on all the interaction between mom and dad—even when it isn't always so pretty—it's a good thing to let them know you have a loving relationship. That doesn't mean you let them witness a flash. But if they should witness a long, intertwined embrace on occasion, better that than a nasty argument.

Why not take up this risqué sport?

French kiss

In Paris I witnessed the most amazing kiss. I spotted two lovers standing on a street corner engaged in the longest lasting French kiss I'd ever seen. The couple didn't emerge for air for over six minutes. I timed it. Their heads swayed from side to side and appeared tilted on an axis veering toward my right. Their embrace reminded me of how sensual two locked lips can be. I'm sure they would have thought I was an obnoxious American for staring if they had looked up, but their eyes never opened. I thought of taking a photo for evidence, but after six minutes of staring, I thought I should walk on.

I remember having those kinds of long, lingering kisses with my husband when he was still my boyfriend. We had make-out sessions in the front seat of his old car that lasted for hours. I remember life before kids when we had idle time. Kissing got top billing. We spent hours trying every variation of head tilts to avoid our noses, and then we'd focus on getting the swirl of our tongues just right. Being married with kids for over ten years has severely affected our kissing. We rarely have time for everlasting kisses.

With our two kids whirling around us constantly I am happy for a French kiss of any length or style. Ours usually last only for 15 seconds on a good day. But seeing this kiss in Paris changed my perspective on the value of a long-lasting French kiss. I placed a long-distance call to my husband right after I saw the kiss to share the news.

I explained in detail how that 6-8 minute kiss transpired. He responded by saying "Well, the guy probably doesn't have kids waking up at the crack of dawn. He's well rested." I said, "We don't know that. Maybe these young lovers just make time for their kisses." But then I thought of my sister's French husband and how since their baby was born they rarely French kiss. She once told me, "Who's got time for that with a two-year-old?"

I said, "But your husband is French!" She said, "Yeah, but we live in the United States!"

Being married in America with kids does not seem to lend itself to unrushed anything. But when I came home I reminded my husband about that Parisian kiss. I expressed my desire for more intimacy amid our hectic life with kids and work. I shared my sense of how I think long-lasting French kisses might add a spark of sensuousness to our state of intimacy. He quietly nodded and murmured, "OK, OK." I realized I would need to take initiative.

These days I don't hesitate. If my husband is near and the kids are at least five feet away, I romance him with a wet, lingering kiss. Even though our lives may not be as carefree as the young lovers I spotted in Paris, I learned an authentic French kiss is always carefree. Ever since my trip across the pond, I French kiss my husband with wild abandon; I'm careful to be carefree.

Break the barriers

For couples with kids, breaking through the barriers to make love is like trying to crush walls made of cast iron, walls that exist in our mind. When we find that stretch of time where it could happen, we choose to be practical instead of impulsive.

Bad move.

Time and energy for lovemaking are rare commodities when you have kids. All the more reason you should seek out all opportunities.

You know what I mean, that unusual evening where you actually get the kids down and still have some energy left. Or that rare afternoon when they're both at Grandma's. Or an anomaly occurs and the kids are mesmerized by a video and you've got 90 minutes of freedom. Or maybe your kids are at the age when they'll actually watch two hours of Saturday morning cartoons if you leave milk and Cheerios on the table.

You could go in your bedroom and lock the door, but do you?

My mind races at these times with hundreds of concerns. I could do a couple of loads of laundry, organize the house, return phone calls, check my e-mail, pay unpaid bills, set up next week's day care, schedule an orthodontic appointment, call the Whirlpool repair person, do my lesson planning for tomorrow, send out overdue thank-you cards.

Anything can fill this precious spot of time, so why not lovemaking? My quest is to reorient my mind toward expressing my love. We have a new motto at our house: "Carpe diem: Make love whenever possible."

After-hours club

Remember when you were really young and you'd stay up until 2 or 3 a.m. with your husband before he was your husband?

Since becoming a mom of two I consider myself lucky if my eyelids are still separated after 9:30 p.m. A wave of sleepiness pulls me like an undertow when I read bedtime stories to the kids. And even if I stay conscious through story time when they ask me for my special mommy tuck-ins, which include cuddling the girls from head to toe, often I submit to sleep by the 20th cuddle. Sometimes I see my husband peeking through the door as my eyes falter and he looks at me longingly as if there's hope for adult conversation, adult love, but sleep often consumes me. I'm usually out by 9:39 p.m., dreaming about a nightlife.

And yet in Paris I learned something new about staying awake. International travel shook my clock to the core. Restaurants don't begin serving dinner until 8 or 9 p.m. Dessert didn't reach my mouth until 10 p.m. The check didn't arrive until 11 p.m. I felt incredibly sleepy by 9 p.m. but had to wait for the meal because I was still hungry. Just when I thought I'd fall asleep; the main course would appear. I kept going like an old car sputtering downhill. By the time we got back to our hotel nightly it was after midnight and I was wired. I stayed up kibitzing with my girlfriends till 1 or 2 a.m.

I was in France for my sister's wedding reception, which took place in a section of a castle. Glorious yet exhausting! Being part of the wedding party truly tested my ability to stay awake. Dinner was served at 10 p.m., dessert at midnight, espresso, special cheeses and cake at 1 a.m. At that point I laid my head on the table and the linen felt like a fine pillow to me, my body surrendering to sleep. That's when my cousin hit me on the shoulder and said, "You have to stay awake . . . . this is your sister's reception. Don't you dare fall asleep." I couldn't fathom drinking espresso at 1 a.m. so I just pushed myself into an upright position and lifted my head off the table. When the dancing began at 1:30 a.m. I moved, I jiggled, I rattled, I swerved. The strobe lights and disco beat pulsed through me. By 2 a.m. my second wind arrived, and by 3:30 a.m. I forgot I was ever tired. My Ah ha moment was when I realized that even I, a mom over 40, could find that second wind.

When I came home I immediately reverted to my old ways and fell asleep by 9:30 p.m. But one night when my husband glanced my way as I began to tuck in the kids, I thought about how I would love a nightlife with him. I thought if I could stay awake past 10 p.m. in France, I could do it once in a while in America. I determined to find my second wind, to see if it could take me to a late night land of passion with my husband. I began an experiment.

One evening after we put the kids to bed I almost fell asleep while tucking in our youngest. My husband caught my eye and said, "Don't go yet." I mustered all my strength, rolled out of her bed, stood up, rubbed my eyes, found my eyeglasses, stubbed my toe on a toy and kept moving toward the living room. I made it.

We talked until 1 a.m. and experienced wild, uninhibited passionate sex, knowing the kids were sound asleep. Blissful. Unusual. Possible. I created an after-hours club with my favorite guy in our own home. With not a peep out of the kids and no calls to answer, we felt like we had a private life for a few hours. We created a married-with-kid's nightlife. Grand.

Neither of us has the stamina for the after-hours club nightly. We have jobs, kids to get to school and pets to feed. But once a month we determine to push, pull, and straggle through that 9:30 p.m. wave of exhaustion and get to the other side. We wake up tired, but humming. I had to cross the Atlantic to find my second wind, but maybe you can catch a current without traveling at all.

Sexual favors

One evening when my husband was completely exhausted I asked him if he would clean the kitchen after dinner. He looked at me and said, "What's in it for me?" I said, "What do you mean? This is part of your job, dude." He then said, "Well how about a little oral sex?" I looked at him as if he'd gone mad, and then said, "Well, if you do the counter tops, the stove top and the fridge, mop the floor and do the dishes, you've got a deal."

When we exchanged vows I could not have fathomed bartering sex for a clean kitchen. But I never knew how exhausting parenting could be. Today I'm ready to cut all kinds of deals for a clean floor, a load of laundry or a foot massage. I'll stoop low for clean silverware. I'm a top-flight negotiator these days.

I know, I know, this seems like prostitution, like bad, bad, bad. But, you know, sometimes it's good to be bad. My husband often has pointed out to me, "Hey, you're my wife. If I can't ask you for what I want sexually, what am I to do?" He's half joking, but he's also half serious.

My 64-year-old father told me something recently that surprised me. I know his wife, my stepmom, often nags him and drives him nuts. So I asked him, "What has kept you guys happily together for more than 25 years now? The sex must be real good," expecting no reply. And he looked directly at me and said, "You know, the funny thing is that, yes, the sex is very good, and you know, honey, that counts for a lot more than you'd imagine." Then he laughed, but it was a serious laugh. He meant it.

And I got it. Sex means a lot to men and women, and we'll put up with noisy kids, poopie diapers, sleepless nights and messy houses with a smile if the sexual favors are happening, but happening good.

Married sex can be great sex

When I was sixteen and going through a gut-wrenching heartbreak breakup I asked my father how he would define true love and he said, "Well, if it's true love, as each year passes, your love continually deepens as you reach new levels of commitment. The sex also gets better because you become closer as time passes."

I wondered if I could ever have that deepening love stuff. And now I do. As I reflect on his comments I realize his definition of true love means that those of us who are married with kids can have great sex!

When I first got married sex was more frequent, but it wasn't necessarily amazing. I wasn't all that comfortable with my husband or myself yet. Over the years as we struggle to parent together, our bonds of trust and comfort have created an interconnectedness that boosts our intimacy to new heights.

For example, as my husband conquers his own negativity to be the best father, I am filled with appreciation, which I express when loving him. This is a particular sentiment that I could only have developed by being a parent with him. It's as if we've been climbing a mountain and though we're tired as hell we get incredible views as we reach new heights.

There's something very intense and mystical about having kids with someone and working together to raise them that creates an incredibly tight type of love. Perhaps it can be a bit constraining at times, but it's also unifying and this unity follows us into the bedroom.

At times it's as if we are one entity. The other night, I heard my husband say, "I love you" and I turned over and muttered, "I love you too honey." He then turned back and said "I never said anything." He declared emphatically that he never said it but that he only thought it. Could we be so connected now that he's telling the truth in that what he thinks I hear him say aloud?

We have the unique advantage that only married life with kids can bring. For instance, he knows and sees daily the constant stress I experience as I deal with the kids. He knows how to help me unwind from that specific stress. When we do make love we know each other so well that he knows exactly how to please me and I, him. He knows me almost better than I know myself, and this makes for the most loving type of sex possible.

As a wife and mother I want more than anything to feel loved for who I am, and this is what my husband is able to express to me. He is not afraid to ask me for what he needs and wants sexually, and I am not nervous about being honest with him. We are developing the type of love the married-with-kids crowd can attain. We share the family life that only makes us stronger and closer as a couple. My Dad was right. True love deepens with time. And if you can have that love, the sex only gets better.

It's OK to be a knockout

I turned a few heads before I had kids. I didn't have the perfect body, but I was happy with it. I felt attractive in my clothes and confident when naked.

When I got pregnant I did all the right stuff, but I still gained 60 pounds. Don't ask me why. I tried to eat healthy food and I swam every day.

I just couldn't help the fact that I craved pastrami sandwiches, knockwurst and Dove bars on a regular basis. The baby was talking to me and my body listened. I couldn't argue with myself. I was only the host body trying to make my guest feel welcome.

Right after the birth of our first daughter, I noticed I lost 9 pounds and I thought: "Wow. Now all I need to lose is 50 more to get back to my pre-birth weight."

When our baby reached three weeks I dared to stare at my body in the mirror. I cried. I saw purplish, silvery stretch marks all over my abdomen, breasts and thighs. I felt like a woman from Star Trek who Captain Piccard or Janeway would glance at and remark, "See the markings. She must be part of an alien race." Even my shoe size increased by an entire size and width. My feet, hips, bladder, breasts, and stomach were forever altered.

My husband loved my body and was attracted to me when I was 50 pounds heavier than normal. He even said he loved my stretch marks and pouchy stomach because it reminded him of where the baby came from. Naturally I appreciated his kind words about my post-birth state.

Nevertheless, I was determined to reclaim the body that was once mine. Regardless of the galactic challenge in front of me, I began pushing my baby in her stroller four miles a day and eating in a low-fat manner. On rainy days I did the Cher exercise videos at home while my baby kept me company in her swing.

It took a year, but I lost the 60 pounds. Gravity shifted my body a bit, but I was at least back to my pre-birth size. In my humble opinion, I could still aspire to be a knockout.

When my husband noticed my metamorphosis he said, "Gee honey, you look great. But you don't need to look that good. You don't need to attract a man. You've got me. Besides, I don't want you to look too good . . . . You're the mother of my children. You're not on the lookout anymore."

Damn him, I thought. What a double standard. I asked him if he would stare at me if I weren't his wife and he said "Definitely. You look hot." I reminded him how he watches what he eats and goes off to work every morning with a splash of cologne and struts off in his leather jacket. He looks hot, and I'm sure women look at him, even though he's a husband and a father.

He quickly realized he was resembling a prehistoric man who wanted his wife to be the Virgin Mary in public, but wanted her to be a sexy broad under his roof. He got the point, and today he's happy that I'm happy with how I look. But for me, it's not just about my outer appearance. It's that I take care of my body and my spirit.

I know that my true beauty comes from within, and the fact that I feel good about myself enhances his attraction towards me. He is more attracted to me and more affectionate toward me today than he was when we first dated. Is my body better than before I had kids? No. But do I feel better about myself and how I take care of myself? You bet.

It feels good to glance at my reflection in a window and smile. As long as I know my true beauty emanates from my spirit, if I want to lose 60 pounds from pregnancy why shouldn't I?

Semiconscious sex

Peg's story

The morning after, I always feel drunk in love.

Spontaneity is a rare thing in marriage, particularly when it happens in the middle of the night. This is what makes semiconscious sex so delicious. Snoring, ever so delicately, I notice my body pulse with passion, a sexual urge, and I wonder what in God's name caused that.

Then I notice, unwittingly, that I'm passionately kissing my husband and I wonder how long has this has been going on. Eventually my husband succeeds in teasing me awake, in rousing me from sleep, but not entirely.

I love these semiconscious sex-capades because they're so sneaky and surprising and the next morning they make fodder for great jokes. "Did I bump into you last night? A couple times?"

Best of all, when the dreaded alarm clock rings, we wake up with a smile and a secret.

And when the routine tumult of the day begins, with the dog and kids to feed, with lunches to pack, with homework to check, now and again it's nice to wake up with a smile and a secret.

Leslie's story

Once in a while we unintentionally deprive ourselves of sex for more than three weeks. At these times a strange phenomenon occurs: semiconscious sex. It happens somewhere between midnight and 4 a.m. We don't plan it. We don't know who initiates it. We don't know how it happens. We don't care. We are just happy to be touching each other.

It's like we are in a dream that startles us into motion. We're so relaxed because actually we're still half-asleep as it's happening. We simply move on urges and physical desires. The conscious part of our brain is completely cut out of the process. Who can think clearly when asleep? We don't. Our bodies take matters into their own hands and decide three weeks is just too long.

Often in the middle of the day when I'm wide awake and nowhere near my husband, I'll think how wonderful it would be to make love to him. But, alas, I am at work, in a store or helping the kids with homework.

When I do see him we're talking with the kids, getting dinner ready and cleaning up after dinner. Or perhaps we're engrossed in a board game with small people. When the kids finally start snoring and we have a chance to be intimate we're often too tired. We tend to opt for sleep or lie still as corpses as if in regeneration capsules preparing for the morning.

If we can't muster the energy for sex while awake, semiconscious sex is the next best thing. The other night we uttered the words: "It would nice to make love." But when we hit the pillows we just wanted sleep. I said, "Let's go to sleep and hope for semiconscious sex to kick in. Goodnight my love."

The rut

Sometimes being married with kids means falling into routines. Periodically my husband and I fall into a sexual rut. It has happened more than once in the last fourteen years. Well, who's counting? The point is, we have finally figured out how to get out of the rut by varying our routines.

Our pattern was to try to have sex after the kids went to bed when we had no energy left. This rarely worked. Without energy or libido it's tough even to take our pajamas off.

The mundane responsibilities of daily life with kids were crushing our creative sexual spirit. After a very dry spell I decided it was time to end this deadlock by being innovative.

One evening while preparing dinner my husband grabbed my butt. At first I pushed his hand away thinking I can't grab him back as we might get interrupted at any moment by our kids. Then I thought, yes, yes! I must use the element of surprise in my favor while I still have some energy.

I grabbed his waist, I kissed his lips, I dropped the vegetables and pulled his body close to mine. The kids never entered the kitchen. Their favorite show was in full swing as we rushed down the hall and locked the bedroom door. Yes, it was quick. Yes, it was passionate. Yes, we broke the routine.

We have discovered what we call pockets of time. The thirty-minute TV show the kids love, the forty five minutes they are at the neighbors playing, the favorite video now showing in the rumpus room.

These days as their favorite show begins I'll grab him and say, "How about now? Right now. We've got a solid fifteen-minute block of time ahead. What do you say?" He'll usually say yes.

The element of unplanned planned sex works for us.

Click, the door locks. Snap, the CD player is on. Flick, a candle is lit. The clothes unbutton, unsnap, and untie. Swish, the curtains are drawn. A few minutes can change everything. We're out of the rut and sensual appetizers make dinner prep a joy.

After we lock the door and close the curtains, we try to rid our minds of mundane thoughts. Once we clear our minds, we strive to be in the moment. We leave our to-do list undone, the dishes in the sink, the doctor's appointment unscheduled. We don't look back, we don't reach ahead, we just try to stay in the moment. Lovemaking, after all, only works in the present tense.

Don't underestimate the power of intimacy. So when you have a spare moment, be impulsive.

We look for opportunities regularly. We persevere. We are opportunists!

Labor delivers

Peg's story

I lay in the hospital bed naked, the sheet tossed aside, resting between contractions.

My doctor walked in, took one look at me and said, "Well, so much for modesty."

I told him that at this point in time I was merely a vessel for this baby, nothing more, nothing less.

My husband, the designated guardian of the "vessel," had as big a role in delivering the baby as I had. He was an extension of me. He took over the control center of my brain, coaxing me to breathe, coaching me to push, filling me with confidence when neither of us had any.

My son was born in a record three hours, and to this day I'm convinced it was my husband who bore that baby. It was his calm, his kindness that kept me moving through it. Luckily he made it back from a trip to France for the birth. I know without him that baby would have had to find another route out of my body. Natural childbirth wouldn't have been an option.

I was in horrendous pain and I wasn't given any pain medicine. I still marvel at how I routinely get more pain medicine at a dentist's office than I was given during child birth. The baby was coming too quickly, the doctor told me.

For couples like us who endure childbirth, who reminisce over colorful war stories, there's a deep connection, one that makes us even more intimate lovers. Because after copiloting excruciating pain, copiloting pure pleasure is second nature. In both scenarios we're an extension of each other where everything rides on trust.

Leslie's story

I clamped my husband in a headlock for three hours straight before our first daughter entered this world. My elbows were clenched so tight around his neck he could barely speak. I screamed, "My butt's gonna break!" The nurses howled back, "Push, push, push. Nothing's gonna break." I limped for six weeks after Tiffany was born. Most of the ligaments near my hip tore. My husband's neck slowly healed and the color returned to his face the next day. Excruciating. And all for love. The love of a child we did not yet know.

When our second daughter was trying to emerge the hospital room was packed. Filled with parents, sisters, nurses and two stressed doctors. I was sweating with both hands pressed firmly on the wall in front of me. My back was arched as I screamed "It's all in my back. My fucking back is in spasm." My husband pushed his entire body weight into his fists and pressed as hard as he could on my lower back for hours as I pleaded "Press harder, harder."

Suddenly, one of the doctors who had recently said "We have a long way to go with these contractions," checked me out and changed his mind. He soon donned a pair of gloves, pulled a rolling chair out of the corner of the room and said to my husband, "Get her on the bed, the baby's crowning." I screamed, "No, I'm not going on the bed, I'm staying standing, I'm not ready, it's not time." The doc replied by looking at Nick and barking "Get her on that bed now!" Nick looked back and forth between the doctor and me as if weighing which decision would get him in the least trouble. Luckily he opted for the medical professional versus me. As if I were as light as a feather, he threw his arms around my 170-pound body and gently threw me into a horizontal position on the bed. Sixty seconds later sweet Marisa came pouring out of me. Nick looked like a vampire had sucked all the blood out of his body as he sighed with relief.

Going through childbirth with my husband changed our relationship forever. His respect and adoration for me deepened in a way only a painful, intense experience like labor can. As each of our daughters came into this planet we bonded through tears of pain and joy. It's as if our love was a bay that flowed into the ocean, venturing into deeper waters.

We were too exhausted to have sex often after the birth of our kids. But when we did the level of intimacy surpassed the type we had experienced before. I remember the first time we had sex after our first daughter was born. The nurse had told us, "Well, you'll need at least 45 minutes of foreplay." My husband balked and we waited eight weeks to build up the stamina to even try.

But when we did get there we were so much more loving towards each other during sex. It was as if we could feel in our skin and bones how much more connected we were now by going through the labor and delivery of our child. We touched each other with such care, respect and appreciation that all senses were heightened.

Making love was truly lovemaking.

Chapter 2

Date your lover

Don't put off dating for two decades

until your kids are conveniently in college

☙

Diversify your portfolio: marital bliss depends on a wealth of babysitters

The world of babysitters is a tough one, filled with competitors.

When someone says, "Oh, can I have your sitter's number?" I quiver, I shake, I hesitate.

I think to myself, are you that good a friend that I should give you such a coveted number? After all, if I give away that number, I could lose my chance for a weekly date with the man I love. I don't know. Do I like you that much as a friend? Do I know you that well?

I tell you, only my best friend gets my sitters' numbers, and only if she agrees not to steal my designated date night.

Now I try to keep sitters on retainer. Will you sit for us every Saturday or every Friday? Can I have first dibs?

If anyone had ever told me that my marital bliss would be dependent upon the availability of teen-age girls, I would have screamed. But who knew about the Family Orbit? Before kids, I lived a different life. I was a free agent, negotiating my terms day by day. Doing what I wanted, when

I wanted. Going places at a moment's notice. No diaper bags, no snacks, no extra clothes, no pacifier, no baby wipes. Who knew?

Our favorite sitter is great, but not only are we dependent upon her availability and her social obligations, but now that she has a boyfriend, we're also dependent on his schedule. For example, I really wanted to go to a staff Christmas party with my husband, but the sitter said, "My boyfriend Josh is off work so I can't sit for you in the evening. I need to be with Josh. But I can watch your kids from 4 to 5:50 p.m." Well, I thought, that's better than nothing. I'll take it.

When I talk to friends who are doing well financially and they tell me, "Oh, I haven't had any time alone with my husband in six months because we just can't find a sitter," I look at them in horror. I feel like saying to each, "Shame on you, you doofus. Are you trying to ruin your relationship? Get out with the guy already."

I'd like to say to my friends, if you put the same amount of energy into finding sitters as you do into your careers and various social obligations, damn right you'd find sitters, and plenty.

There's a Japanese word called "Ichinen" and it means determination and how your entire life is oriented. If you're oriented toward nurturing your marriage, the entire universe can line up to support you.

I'm not launching a dotcom, but I am trying to maintain the start-up I began 13 years ago: my marriage. It's a valuable commodity in the course of my lifetime, and spending time alone with my investment can make a difference.

So do the prep work in order to date your spouse. Diversify that babysitter portfolio. Collect babysitter names wherever you go. Get references.

Network, network, network.

Weekly date nights are not expendable

Cardinal Rule No. 1: Date nights are not superfluous or expendable. When I got married no one ever told me how crucial it would be to date my husband. The only clue I ever had that life after kids could cause my relationship to crumble was when my Mom said, "Yeah, people usually get divorced after they have kids. That's what happened to your Dad and me. After you three came along, we had no time for our relationship."

I remember thinking, oh Mom's just being so negative, so pessimistic, so ridiculous. Children will bring us closer than ever. What did I know?

After our first daughter was born I discovered something called "colic." Being with a fussy, crybaby all day changed me. I turned into a worn, wicked witch of a wife. When my husband came home I didn't want to talk or even look at him. I couldn't fathom doing anything for anyone else. As soon as he walked in that door I passed off the baby and said with all my being, "Leave me alone. And, oh, if you're hungry, go fix yourself something. I'm spent."

I remember thinking, "I'm in baby prison. Get me out of here." A friend told me, "You're headed for trouble in your marriage." Then she made a concrete suggestion that sounded simple, yet wise. She said, "No matter what, you have to go out on a date with your husband once a week, even if it's only for an hour, two hours, whatever. Trade with a friend, beg your family for help, find a babysitter, but at all costs do it or you'll lose your relationship and fast."

At first I thought, I can't leave this infant even for an hour, and then I thought, well, maybe I can. Maybe my relationship is worth nurturing, Oh, who am I kidding? I've got to nurture my marriage.

Date nights have saved us by enabling us to stay close amid the stress of work, babies and life. I still like the guy, because every week over the past nine years we've taken the time to look each other in the eye and say, "How are you? Who are you?" We've taken the time to have at least one uninterrupted meal a week where the table stays clean. Where the linens are white. Where there's nothing sticky all around us. Where we can actually complete a thought.

One of my girlfriends said recently, "You know, Leslie, maybe if I had started dating my husband 10 years ago when we married we could have made it. We basically loved each other and have had no huge arguments over the years. But it feels too late now. We don't know each other anymore. The love and sweetness that was once there is gone and there's no way to get it back. I don't care about him anymore. We haven't spent time alone together in 10 years. But we have the big house, the two kids, and we make a lot of money. We're going to a counselor to figure out how to separate. I'll probably lose the house and have to share custody."

Certainly dating your spouse won't solve all marital problems, but it can help you keep your emotional connection. Sometimes spending time alone together without the kids is really all we need to keep a loving feeling between us.

For far too many of us, it's a novel idea to date our spouse, to spend time alone with him/her weekly in a romantic setting, one that doesn't require us to cook, mop up spills or break up fights.

The 15-minute rule

I never knew how completely exhausted my bones could be until I had a 2-year-old and an infant while holding down a teaching job. In those days, as soon as we'd get the babies to sleep, my husband, Nick, and I would immediately want to vegetate. We'd end up staring at the TV for an hour or so. We didn't talk to each other. We barely acknowledged each other's existence. We barely made it down the hall to our bed, and we barely uttered a word before falling asleep.

It went on like this for a while. Sometimes it would vary. After the kids went down one of us would watch TV while the other would take a phone call, get on the computer, clean the kitchen floor. But we didn't talk. We were too wiped out to give anything to each other.

After a year of this, one night I sat up in bed at 2 a.m. and started crying. He said, "Oh, no, I don't have the energy for this kind of heavy talk at 2 a.m. We've got to get up early. Let's talk later."

I looked at him and said, "There is no later in our world. I need to tell you that I feel so alone, so isolated, so sad, so trapped by my obligations to the family. It's like we're roommates and I feel so alone."

The strangest thing happened just then. He sat up and looked at me and started to cry. He said, "Well, you know, I feel exactly the same way. I feel trapped by my obligations, alone and disconnected from you."

We both realized that we had to become each other's best friend. We knew one thing for sure. The kids were not going to solve this problem for us. We needed to become allies or risk losing each other with two kids under the age of 5.

That's when we started the 15-minute rule.

Here's how it works. After we get the kids to bed—before we pick up that phone, touch a computer key, hit that TV remote or load the dishwasher—we sit down and we look at each other's face and we talk for at least 15 minutes every night, no matter what. (Barring a major flu, of course.)

We talk about our day, our struggles, our challenges, what we ate for lunch, anything we want. But we each get a turn to talk and to listen.

We talk to each other for 15 minutes every day, and while this may not seem like a long time, people who live in a family filled with play dates, jobs, soccer, homework and P.T.A. meetings know that to have an uninterrupted 15-minute conversation is something of a small miracle.

At times it's a strain to keep our eyes open, but we talk until we have a chance to connect. During this time we typically sit close together. We're almost like two trained seals now who huddle up into a 15-minute pose once the kids go to bed.

We began this several years ago and we have rarely felt isolated or trapped since. It may not be a cure-all to talk daily, but it has greatly improved our relationship.

Of course it's a policy that requires some discipline. If I slip up and touch that remote or try to hide on the couch in front of an "I Love Lucy" rerun, Nick will come into the room and say, "Hey, aren't you going to talk to me? What about the 15-minute rule?" Or if Nick gets in that really comfy position on the living room couch and I see him going down for the count, I nudge him and say, "Hey aren't we going to talk about our day?" Or if there's a hot basketball game on I'll say "Hey, what about the 15-minute rule?" And he'll say, "Oh I guess I can just catch that last quarter.

"Let's talk."

Salsa Sundays

Something magical happens when you dance with your partner, when the lights are low, when the kids are with a sitter and you can't talk about anything practical or domestic. With the music so loud, you can barely utter a word. All you can do is look at each other and concentrate on your dance steps. You have to put every ounce of your energy into ensuring you don't step on each other's feet . . . especially if one of you is wearing open-toe shoes.

For years during our date night my husband and I would go out to dinner, to a movie or maybe a play, but eventually it got a bit old. Sedentary activity is nice, but the thought of actually moving together, doing something physical, yet not too strenuous, intrigued me. I asked him, "Is there any type of dance lesson you would consider taking with me?" "Only salsa," he said. I quickly found a place in town with lessons, and that was that.

It took us a year of weekly classes to learn how to dance with each other, to sense each other's rhythm, but once we got it we took off.

When he holds me in his arms and steers me to the left and to the right, I feel interconnected with each of his moves. The dance instructor yells out: "Let the man lead. When you're at home do what you want, but when you're here let the man lead." We laugh, but we know she means it. We move our hips and joints together to the salsa cow—bell with a huge smile on our faces. As we rub up against each other, I am aroused by this husband of mine who seems unlike a married man with kids, but simply my hot Latin lover on the dance floor.

Now we not only dance when we're out, but we also dance at home. Often, before dinner he'll put on the salsa CD, grab my arm and start spinning me around, wooden spoon in hand, pasta sauce dribbling on the floor. Now we scoot around the living room at a moment's notice and often find ourselves dancing for 15 to 20 minutes while the kids watch their favorite PBS show, "Arthur."

On the nights we go out to salsa, I look forward to dressing up. Likewise, I look forward to seeing my husband in shirts without kid stains.

Dancing revives the couple in us; it's when we forget for several hours each week that we're parents with a mortgage, unpaid bills and teachers with prep to do.

When our only worry is stepping out of step.

No formal attire required: Just renew your vows yearly

Leslie's story

The kids came roaring into the house with my husband during our most recent anniversary, and our little one said, "Mommy, Mommy stand on the X in the living room." When a 5-year-old gives you a command with such fervor—you listen. I didn't know what was up, but I decided I better go and stand on the X. As I stood there our 9-year-old said, "Mommy, here's the card." And then my husband got down on his knees about four feet in front of us and presented me with a new ring. His card brought us all to tears because in it he said he wanted to renew our vows.

I fell in love once more.

That was our 12th anniversary, but we renew our vows yearly. We go away overnight and celebrate our love and our determination to take care of our relationship. During one anniversary my husband made this toast: "Let's change our karma." I thought this was an odd statement and asked why he made it. He simply said, "Well, both our parents are divorced and maybe we have this karmic tendency in our own lives. Let's vow to change our karma and not repeat the mistakes they made. Let's determine to stay happily married despite the obstacles."

"O.K.," I said. "I'll toast to that."

Peg's story

My husband, Tim, says the Chinese language sounds like hot butter slowly sizzling on the skillet.

With this sizzling chatter as a backdrop, we sat in the garden of the Forbidden City in Beijing and renewed our vows.

It was a simple affair. No dress rehearsal. All we did was take off our rings and said some sweet words about each other and our marriage. Then we put our rings back on and felt a dimension closer.

It happens every time we renew our vows.

What I like about renewing marriage vows is that unlike the pomp and circumstance of a wedding, it's a modest doing, an intimate gathering of two. It's especially fun to do this abroad because you're surrounded by strangers. In our case, sweet, sizzling strangers.

To celebrate a previous anniversary we renewed our vows at Notre Dame in Paris before a beautiful stained glass window. Someone heard that we were planning to get remarried and asked, "How does one put on a wedding at Notre Dame?"

I laughed at the absurdity of reserving Notre Dame, draping it in flowers and inviting hundreds of family members to attend. No, we prefer to renew our vows in the company of strangers. (Of course, we actually think of them as thousands of free witnesses.)

Marriage is a bond that grows deeper over time . . . that is, as long as you renew it with some regularity.

A book club for two

Reading a book with my husband gives us a special connection, a means of reaching beyond everyday issues and delving into philosophy, wisdom, ethics, ideas. This is a rare thing for harried parents whose topics of conversation too often are limited to the fundamentals of living: grocery lists, car pools, homework. Sharing a book is a good way to stay connected, because even though our conversations about it may be interrupted, we can still share thoughts on the same plane.

When my husband and I went to Maui we packed up our daughter, then 2, and all of her accessories, and still managed to take along two copies of "Jurassic Park" in our loot. This was back in 1993, before the movie was out, but it was a much-anticipated film. We decided it would be fun to read the book at the same time and join the masses "anticipating."

We never officially designated ourselves a book club for two, but I can tell you that this "unnamed" club was enormous fun. We were challenged to keep pace with each other and the book was so suspenseful that it was a race to the end. I lost sleep because I couldn't stop reading; the end of every chapter was a cliffhanger.

Reading books with my husband also has been a good model for my kids, who notice when we're both spellbound by the same book. Now my daughter and I are in a mother-daughter book club, as well, and the experience has made us closer.

Clearly, books are an adventure for people to share. I've heard some couples like to read poetry to each other, a sweet way of being together, listening to words from an intimate voice.

So far we have just delved into the genre of suspense. And if you're a fan of thrillers, you know how they take over your life. They consume you; they're all you can talk about for a stretch of time.

It's fun to be consumed by a book with a consumed spouse.

The getaway

Parenting with minimal down time requires parents to make good on the 24-hour getaway once or twice a year. Seems impossible, I know. That's what I thought, too. How can I leave my nursing infant and demanding toddler for what seems like a luxury, an option no longer within reach in my kid-populated household?

During those early years when my children jockeyed for my attention, squeezing my husband into my schedule was a challenge. But a wise friend insisted I make the 24-hour getaway standard policy in my home. She told me, "It's a must. Find a way."

I thought it sounded ridiculous but, once we did it, it made all the sense in the world. For the past nine years we have had our yearly 24-hour getaways, and they have revived our marriage every single time. Once we figured out the logistics—pumped the breast milk, packed the backpack, front pack, and portable crib for the caregiver—we made our escape.

And during every getaway, that unhurried time away has felt timeless. I notice that an hour seems like three hours, a minute seems like 10. Our meals seem to linger. Likewise our conversation. Our intimacy, heightened.

To know that I have a stretch of 24 hours ahead of me is almost as great as the time itself.

As we drive off alone in the car and take that first deep breath, the kind you know won't be interrupted by a crying child demanding food or comfort, I look back at the house where we leave the kids and I worry for a split second, and then I sigh.

As we turn on our favorite music—not the Wee Sing tape or the Britney Spears CD—it dawns on us that we are utterly and completely alone in the car together. We both feel as though we're debriefing from an intense CIA mission. After about an hour of downloading pertinent information, we finally start to relax.

Then I begin to remember what it's like to be alone with this person, and I remember how and why I fell in love with him. I feel carefree and almost youthful again. For now, for right now, I'm only responsible for big people.

As we walk toward the front desk to check in, I look at him and notice how carefree he is when he's not tending to the needs of two small children, a dog and a fish. And when he has untapped energy to devote to me it's so decadent . . . so lovely . . . so rare.

When we're alone in the hotel room staring at the ocean after making unrushed love, he asks me if I'd like anything to drink, a question he rarely has time to ask me at home. I say "Yes, some Calistoga water with a twist of lemon would be great." He caters to me like when we were first dating, and after all these years, it's nice to be a date.

When we head back to pick up the kids, we're usually a bit quiet on the drive. We know we're re-entering the Family Orbit, and we do so with caution. And yet, we're well prepared for the jolt of children. We're refreshed and revitalized because time away makes our relationship sweeter and stronger.

If you want to have a healthy marriage, if you want to stay connected to your spouse, once or twice a year plan to date him/her for 24 hours in a row.

It's non-negotiable.

Cell phone romance

My husband and I cellered up for the same reason most American couples purchase cell phones: safe travel, track kids' whereabouts, help kids track our whereabouts.

Today we'd add to that list: cell phone romance.

Before we joined the cell mania populace, neither of us realized how much romance a cell phone could possess. We found out after we bought the family plan, which allows husband and wife limitless calls for free. Now my husband and I call each other several times during the day just to kibitz. Sometimes we have a joke we want to try out on each other. Sometimes we're just looking for a little company.

We have always checked in with each other on routine matters: car pool pick-up, last-minute grocery store detail. But before we were official cell phone owners, we called each other at work and we had to act professional or risk someone at the next cubicle hearing a randy joke.

But when you're driving in your car, one hand on the wheel, the other on cell, you're as free as the wind. It's these kind of free-spirited communiqués with your spouse that make for cell phone romance.

These sweet, spontaneous, racy conversations remind me of when my husband and I moved across the country, each driving a separate car in tandem with a headset walkie—talkie on to keep track of each other.

The funny thing is that we did much more than keep track of each other. We humored each other with jokes. We impersonated people. We commented on how stunned we were to see a real live tumbleweed on the side of the road in Amarillo, Texas. We talked each other down the Manzano Mountains during a snowstorm, keeping pace with each other down steep, winding roads to safety in Albuquerque, New Mexico. We later acted like racecar commentators, reporting that one of us was in front, while the one in the rear was inching up.

Our communiqués were fun and playful and humorous and comforting and sweet. We, quite simply, kept each other company.

With children in the house, one-on-one conversations are rare and require effort. Four-on-four conversations, which are the norm, are void of off-color remarks and sexual innuendoes. Sometimes you find yourself wondering: "Where is that funny, outrageous man I married?"

You simply miss his company.

You see, when you fall in love you may think that you're in love with someone's smile or quick wit or philosophical view of life. But what you're actually in love with is the whole package: his company.

Fooling around on the cell phone is a way to conjure up that pre-kid romance. And this is key because when you become a parent you become a co-manager of children in a busy house where intimate conversations with your mate are rare. It's best to think of ways to keep each other company off premises.

Our cell phone communiqués, our free-spirited snippets of conversations, give us more air time. And when the cell phone companies discover cell phone romance, expect them to start marketing cell phone rendezvous packages.

The honeymooners

The word "Honeymoon" conjures up many images for me. Jackie Gleason arguing with his wife, yelling "To the moon!" Lovers caressing each other in public. Having long talks while lying around naked. Bliss.

Deciding to revisit the place where we spent our honeymoon was a wise decision. During the trip my heart opened slowly like the petals of a flower wound too tight.

Daily life with children rarely allows us time to reflect on the last hour much less the last decade. After 14 years of marriage we took a long weekend to reminisce. Even on our wedding day we joked about having kids and what their names might be. But we had never spent more than a few hours with a person under the age of ten. We had no idea what impact children would have on our lives.

As we drove the winding roads toward our honeymoon spot the wind whipped my hair across my eyes. I closed my lids and recalled what it was like to be newlyweds walking along the beach. When I saw the sun-kissed Mendocino coastline I felt 29 again.

I caught my face in the rear-view mirror and I smirked at myself as I noticed the lines near my brow, eyes and lip area that only 14 years of laughing, crying and worrying as a parent could bring.

I glanced at my husband and grabbed his hand, filled with appreciation for our kids and even the stress in our lives. I squeezed his fingers tight as the sun bounced off his gold band. I sighed. We still like each other. We've even accepted the minivan as a staple in our lives.

During the past decade of life with kids we have learned to forgive each other for our faults. We also have developed the ability to treat each other with patience and kindness, even when the kids push us to the outer edges of exhaustion.

During the first years of our marriage I had almost no patience with my husband and so little trust in his decisions. Today our love is much stronger; I think we have honed the qualities of patience and trust by parenting together. Our kids have been our teachers.

As we entered the cottage we stayed at more than a decade earlier we laughed because we barely remembered the layout. We lit a fire, unloaded our lingerie loot and had a private fashion show.

We appreciated the room ten times more than we did during our honeymoon. The view from the deck seemed much more spectacular. Our perception had shifted to one of deep appreciation. We felt like navy officers who had earned their stripes.

Later we indulged in a fancy dinner and stared at each other like we were on a first date. As we awaited our meal I noticed a matchbox that listed the number 1-888-IN-LOVE. The matchbook made me grin, as it seemed a wise token symbolizing how we can keep our passion burning. We vowed to return to this hot spot every few years.

The next morning we hiked along the sandy beach cliffs and held each other tight. We sipped coffee and lollygaged around the town like two people with no where to go. We tickled each other and fondled each other's hair like we did eons ago when time was not so precious.

We had only a few days at our honeymoon digs, but it felt like a month. I'll never underestimate the value of retracing those steps.

When we arrived back home we stepped into sibling rivalry. The kids were arguing at top volume. The dog was barking, and the parakeet perched on my head. But I was smiling inside.

As I blinked, I visualized the sun shimmering across the ocean in front of that cottage that sits along the Mendocino bluffs, awaiting our return.

Chapter 3

Be Kind to Your Lover

Even grown-ups need to be nurtured

☙

Remember the Prime Point

At 4 a.m. when your baby is stirring and you and your spouse begin your ritual raucous debate over whose turn it is to tend to the baby . . . when you begin to see red only to have your searing coherent arguments drift into a muddle of sleep talking, it probably doesn't occur to you why in God's name you married this man or woman in the first place.

This seemingly elusive reason is what we call the PRIME POINT, the "reason" we fell for X. Perhaps it was his compassion, his sense of fun or his sheer sense of adventure. But the prime point is even more involved than that. It's the reason we chose this particular person with whom to spend our entire life. It's the reason we decided to make a commitment and take a leap of faith, trusting we would fall deeper in love over time.

Of course baby-rearing is a hard regimen, and a person once buoyed by humor can seem humorless, even grouchy for days at a time. But you can't measure a spouse's true merit without factoring in the prime point. You simply have to give him or her some slack and recall those carefree, spontaneous days B.C. (Before Children).

We have to come to grips with the fact that children change a person's spirit. For the most part, it's a new, improved spirit. Parents are blessed with a source of unconditional love in the form of chirping babies. But there is one harsh reality, and that is parents are never really carefree in the same way. This can take a toll on some, and so you have to make some allowances for your spouse.

When you begin to consider your spouse a strange bedfellow, you need to remind yourself of the prime point. Sometimes, during a particularly challenging stretch of parenting, you may even have to do this exercise a few times a day. You won't be sorry because the prime point will help you peel away all the layers of stress that have put all those concerned creases in your spouse's forehead.

And before long you'll begin to recognize your long-lost spouse or, more accurately, recall the best part of him or her. Once you factor in the prime point, you begin to realize the value of your memory's eye.

Salt your spouse's plate

Awise old woman once said you should be so nice to your husband, that when he's eating dinner you should have the kindness to say, "Would you like a little bit more salt on that, honey?"

Ridiculous.

Or that's what the young woman thought who had sought out the wise woman's advice. What can a mom, depleted from the yelps of a baby, hope to give her husband? Nothing is the sane answer.

But the wise woman argued. She said that instead of worshipping the baby, a wife should be really kind and considerate to her husband. Always put that relationship first. Otherwise what is the point of having children, anyway?

I venture to say that if this wise old woman had been a wise young woman, she would have said each spouse should be so nice to each other that they salt each other's plate.

This image makes me smile. I often think of it when I'm trying to keep my marriage a priority with a little one nipping at my heels. It isn't easy. There are times I'd like to tell my dear husband to look after himself. After all, I already have child dependents.

But that's not the way it works in the best of families. The best of families are based on the trickle-down theory. In short, when Mom and Dad are united, goodwill trickles down to the children. When Mom and

Dad take care of their relationship, taking care of the children falls into place.

The truth is, we parents are overwhelmed by the family unit and, sadly, instead of pulling together as a couple, we all too often lose sight of each other . . . for years.

We work too many hours. We forget to date each other. We even forget to talk to each other, aside from briefings on carpool schedules and what's for dinner.

Somehow, in the midst of bringing up baby, we can't muster the energy to have those deep meandering talks that last until 4 a.m. about the meaning of life and favorite one-liners. We simply forget to be with each other. And after years of failing to salt each other's plate—we can lose the best part of us as a couple.

It seems to us that if all couples had the fortune of hearing this wise woman and her point-blank blunt comments, they would realize that if they decide to have children it will be a challenge to hold on to each other—but nothing insurmountable.

People make a mistake when they conclude their spouse no longer needs tender loving care once they have a house full of kids. When you tend to your loved one and he or she tends to you, before you know it, you're both well tended.

As for the children? When Mom and Dad salt each other's plate, they salt everybody's plate.

A paradigm shift

We are the generation hell-bent on getting this parenthood thing down. We've sworn off our parents' mistakes, read parenting books and consulted with counselors at the first sign of trouble.

We are determined to keep our offspring off the psychologist's couch. But we may well be putting too much energy into keeping our children on track . . . that is, if it creates an energy deficit with our spouse.

I made a mistake early on in our marriage when I decided that since my husband was a big person, he could fend for himself. I made my daughter my first priority and focused on her needs.

Now I see that this thinking is flawed. It's not a question of priorities. It's a question of energy. A paradigm shift in parenting comes when a person realizes that families run on energy, not priorities. If you put all your energy into your children, you won't have the energy reserves for your spouse, no matter how deeply you care for him/her.

So if you have a policy of "Children First" at your house, you should rethink it. When parents are too devoted to their kids, a space can grow between couples, and if untended, it can become a chasm.

Lots of couples lose touch over this one, so do a little family inventory. Do you engage your spouse in conversations with as much enthusiasm as your children? Do you consider your spouse's feelings as often as you do those of the kids'? Do you save energy for your spouse every day or do you meet up with him/her at the end of the day when you are depleted?

If you scored high for spousal displacement, make a paradigm shift in parenting and strive to balance your energy output.

My husband is Type A, I'm Type Z

Perhaps you secretly suspect you're Type Z.

For the record, Type Zs are directionally challenged, disorganized and perpetually late. They lollygag through life, don't think to wear a watch and are always in the doghouse for mismanaging time.

You can trust me on the Type Z profile because I've been in the doghouse for years.

My Type A husband is often in a snit because he says he spends half his life waiting for me.

I was late before I had kids, but now I'm even less reliable. That's because with kids I'm traveling through time with unpredictable delays far worse than mechanical failures or poor weather conditions. A tantrum alone can hold you up seven minutes, and that's not counting the cleanup involved with scattered toys and wayward crackers. Count on 15 minutes for convincing a kid that going to school stark naked is probably not the best idea.

Children are hard to keep on track, and Type Zs like me regularly lose touch with that basic fact. We plow through life running our usual

5 minutes behind and are always astonished when our children steer us further off course, making our time of arrival a virtual crapshoot.

Type As, on the other hand, are meticulous planners of time, tracking it on spreadsheets and Palm Pilots. They are efficient and can be credited for factoring in the whimsy of children. But for all their efficiency, they lack compassion when Type Zs show up late. They can't imagine how a person can move through the day watchless.

When my husband, Tim, and I recently packed the kids up for a family reunion, our Type A/Type Z tendencies clashed. Tim began packing days ahead of time, turning down a night out at the movies just to make sure he had enough organization time.

I, on the other hand, didn't start packing until the night before, pulling a virtual all-nighter, sadly scoring only 5 hours of sleep before our 4 a.m. wake-up call.

On another occasion we had a good laugh at our Type A/Type Z disparity. We took the kids into San Francisco for the day and Tim pulled money out of his wallet for the tollbooth miles before we ventured across the Golden Gate Bridge.

He commented that if I were driving, I probably wouldn't search for cash in my billfold until I reached the tollbooth, slowing traffic. True enough.

Of course our extremes are even more extreme in the kitchen. One time we were getting ready to have a couple over for dinner. Tim spent the night before prepping the main course. I, on the other hand, began making a pie one hour before they were to arrive.

My Type A husband tried to talk me out of it, but Type Zs actually like a challenge, so I opted to bake like a bat out of hell. Ten minutes before they were to arrive I finished the pie, but the kitchen was a disaster, and I felt like pigpen in a cloud of flour.

I cleaned up in record time, and when the guests arrived at the front door I slipped out the back and around to the side door. I rushed upstairs, snuck a five-minute shower, slipped on a dress, applied 2.3 minutes worth of makeup and arrived at my dinner party only 10 minutes late looking great.

My husband was the most surprised. He said: "Dear, somehow you really pulled this one off. It just goes to show you, you should never estimate a Type Z. Never overestimate a Type Z. Never underestimate a Type Z. Because with a Type Z, you never know what you're going to get."

Now that we've finally identified ourselves as Type A and Type Z, we seem to make more jokes and fewer snide remarks. Of course identifying ourselves wasn't easy because my profile seemed in flux. You see, I'm Type A at work and Type Z at home. But we concluded that the trick to profiling yourself is to determine what type you are at home.

In the end, most couples are a union of Type A and Type Z. These couples annoy the hell out of each other, but they're together for a reason.

Type A is the compass and Type Z is the adventurer. Both deserve equal status, although cohabiting in a house full of children can be a rude awakening.

Here are some crucial tips to keep you happily married with kids:

1. Type As should never criticize Type Zs about their time management, but rather offer polite suggestions.
2. Type Zs should try to remind themselves that children never move in a straight line and if they have a lunch date, it's a good idea to drive there right after breakfast.
3. Type As should buy Type Zs waterproof watches.
4. Type Zs should try to remember to wear their waterproof watch.
5. Type As should endeavor to be patient, and to remember that it's in children's nature to meander. Rushing them unmercifully may be more time-consuming, as they resist being bullied.
6. Type Zs should never agree to meet someone at a designated time but rather insist on a flexible, 30-minute window.
7. Type Zs should try to do one thing that is responsible every day. Maybe two.
8. Type As should try to do one thing that is utterly spontaneous every day. Three on Saturday.

Finally, Type As and Type Zs should appreciate their differences and remind themselves that being opposites is a good thing. This way couples won't stray too far off course when they lollygag.

Dream and dare your spouse to dream

A lifetime is a colorful journey. No doubt there are going to be uncertain career paths, layoffs, intolerable jobs, inhumane bosses. And, yet, when you're a parent it's tough to afford yourself the luxury of dreaming. You can be overwhelmed by real-life worries: the mortgage, braces, day-care costs, etc.

Even so, I'm convinced that dreaming is the best financial security because, in the end, the only real security in life is happiness. There's no way to protect yourself from a layoff, a demotion or a hostile work environment. When you think it through, security is really just "peace of mind," and the only way to secure your peace of mind is to make sure you're happy.

So when one member of the couple is having a rough time, it's a good idea to remind him/her to make an appointment to dream.

Ask your spouse how he/she would like to spend each day. Break it down hour by hour. Very insightful. Then challenge your spouse with this one: If you're not on your path, you're off it. Follow that pithy line with my uncle's favorite: It takes a long time to be an overnight success.

So true. Those famous people on the talk show circuit may be billed as an overnight success, but those of us who know the true meaning of success realize that success really takes determination, energy and the willingness to fail. More than likely those "overnight successes" have spent years on projects that, in the end, were less than successful. And yet they never gave up because they didn't see failure in the traditional sense. They saw failure as merely a wrong turn, and a helpful cue to the right one.

So encourage your spouse to dream, big dreams, lofty dreams, complicated dreams, convoluted dreams.

If you can't convince your spouse to dream for the fun of it, use the "sensible" approach. Tell him or her that the best way to safeguard security is to safeguard happiness. Remind your spouse that six-digit salaries and stock options do not ensure happiness. If he/she needs proof, point to the recent wave of laid-off dotcom execs who bailed out of business to join the Peace Corps.

Dreaming may seem frivolous, but it's anything but. It's a reliable compass to search out happiness.

Seduce your spouse with humor

When I first dated my husband, I thought he was hilarious because he had such witty one-liners. At the time I wasn't much of a film buff, so I didn't realize that he was stealing one-liners from Hollywood and in actuality I was falling in love with a thief.

But it wasn't long before I became sophisticated enough in film noir to call his bluff and demand he footnote these clever lines.

To be honest, I'm just as dishonest. While I don't steal my material from movies, I pickpocket it from unsuspecting people I cross paths with—colleagues, family and friends. (I prefer humor you can't trace.)

Over time I have amassed a great collection of one-liners to weave into everyday conversation. With a select few I can get my spouse howling.

Humor in the house is important, even more so when you have children padding about. A house with children is a busy house, and a busy house is often a stressful house. Humor is the comic relief of which the married-with-kids crowd is in dire need.

So if you want to seduce your spouse with humor, you're welcome to some of my most favorite, stolen lines:

"Everyone has their IDIOT-syncrasies."

"You are odd, even."

"You are my damsel causing stress."

"The only thing those pet chickens of yours need is a good marinade."

"There's this man I see every day, and he's always so happy. He always has this big smile on his face. What's his problem? What's he so happy about? He's either really stupid or really shallow."

"I told him (my new boyfriend) we're not going steady; we're going steadily."

"I like fromage, but I don't like cheese."

"My wife likes to talk. She won't take silence for an answer."

"She's left of Lenin. He's right of Attila the Hun."

"She cares about the human race. She just wants to win."

Grandma Mary's rule

Never ever put your spouse down in front of others.

If you have something negative to say, something that's bothering you, something to criticize, do it when you're alone with your mate, not in front of family, friends, co-workers or even the bank teller. No matter how tempting, wait until you're alone.

My Grandma Mary said that when you put your mate down in front of others, it compounds and intensifies the put-down by at least 50 percent. Wait until you can talk privately, even if it means waiting hours or days until you can get a private moment. No matter how tempting, wait until you're alone.

I still have to discipline myself to take this advice.

When I want to get a dig in about a pet peeve or something my husband has been doing that annoys me, it's easy to throw it out at a family function and get my siblings or my girlfriends to rally behind me. But this not only makes him feel terrible, it creates a bigger problem than might have existed originally.

My husband will use this ugly put-down tactic in front of friends when he has home remodeling ideas that he knows I don't agree with, something we've battled about. He'll mention it in front of friends to rally support for his cause or to insinuate that I have no sense of taste. This never works for him anyway, even if friends and family side with him at the time. We always go back to the drawing board, but the putdown makes the issue much more charged and much more personal.

The cruelest put-down of all, of course, is when a spouse puts us down in front of our children. This one is hard to forgive, and it creates a multitude of problems, some irreversible.

Grandma Mary knew how powerful and unwieldy words could be. She didn't believe there was a place for public humiliation in a marriage.

Love is a verb

God never intended love to be passive, even though most people ponder love rather than practice it.

They sit around and try to measure the beat of their heart, especially when it's palpitating. They make hopeless comments like: "I just don't think I have feelings for X anymore. The love is gone."

These ponderers are missing the point. If someone had feelings for another once, chances are those feelings can be resuscitated. Naturally, there are some exceptions to the rule . . . tragic love stories that involve physical or emotional abuse. Those cases do require mind over matter.

But what I'm talking about here is when love seems desolate, when both parties have been so inattentive to each other that both feel utterly unattended. And yet, instead of sitting back, these couples should do some tending. They should initiate a call, a date, a romantic interlude, whatever.

I have always believed that love is a practice, and I suppose that's why I became a policy wonk romantic when I first got married. I initiated the birthday breakfast-in-bed policy, now law in our home.

The idea was for each of us to make the other breakfast in bed for a week to celebrate our birthdays. I never thought of it as a particularly exhausting practice because breakfast can mean a Pop-Tart and cereal, right?

Wrong.

When I first served my food and wine connoisseur a Pop Tart and Cheerios, he balked. My husband decided to make these breakfasts upscale. He started serving eggs benedict, and champagne in a flute with a strawberry in it. You get the idea. He's a classy guy with a competitive edge.

Naturally I couldn't take that kind of treatment sitting down. I was determined to out-breakfast my husband, plotting new recipes, searching out new breakfast cookbooks, fine-tuning my German pancakes, etc.

My sister teased me, and while she stopped short of calling me a romantic rookie, she intimated that all this frivolity would end when we had kids because life would get too busy.

She was right, to a degree. We don't get a streak of seven breakfasts in bed anymore. We're actually lucky to get two, but they're still lovely, even though we have to pile extra food on the tray for the kids who hop in bed with us and demand their fair share. The whole affair is messier, with syrup dribbling on the sheets, but what the hell? After 15 years we're still at it and we're both still enormously competitive.

My husband, I'm certain, is in it for the decadent breakfasts, the fierce competition and the long-standing joke of it all. I'm in it for all that, sure, and one thing more. It's a great way to practice love.

Sometimes listen to your spouse

I'll never forget the day my husband came home from work and said, "I'm just a slave for you and Tiffany." Our daughter was then an infant. I could not believe my ears. I refused to hear him. Several weeks later I probed. "What did you mean you're just a slave for Tiffany and me?"

He explained how he hated his job but felt there was no way out. He had to continue climbing under buildings and retrofitting structures to earthquake-proof them so that I could stay home with the baby. I was horrified. How could he think this way? I could not be the cause of anyone feeling like a slave, could I?

I spoke with a good friend who said, "Try listening to what he's saying. Perhaps you need to offer him some options. Let him know you will support him for a while if he needs to make a career change."

This was not what I wanted to hear while my 2-month-old lay sleeping. But I must admit that I needed to try to listen not only to what I wanted to hear, but to what he was trying to say. It was tough for me, because I always thought my ideas were better, my opinion more valid. I thought it made more sense for me to focus on the baby. So what if he had to suffer a bit on the job?

Had I really become a self-centered wife so fast? Well, I realized my friend was right. Sometimes it's important to listen to your husband. I decided to muster my courage and say, "Honey, I'll go back to work full time so that you can get retrained and change careers if you want to. I want you to be happy."

I was able to work part time while he went back to school to become a teacher. It was the first step in the right direction for our marriage. I began to listen to him more and actually hear him. Our relationship became much more loving and filled with mutual respect. He shined because he was being heard and he expressed much more affection toward me.

I used to think I had all the answers. What did I know about listening? Marriage for us is a constant exercise in trying to really hear each other.

Quick tips on how to be a better listener:

1. Make sure you create a time to listen. Send the kids to bed (or out of the house, if necessary). Whatever it takes, carve out some quiet time so you can really listen to your spouse.
2. Try to free your mind of other things. Avoid creating mental grocery lists while your spouse is speaking. Don't plan the rest of your day in your head during the dialogue.
3. Remember that you are your spouse's best friend. Act like one. Listen with an "I love you" attitude.
4. Try to think of yourself in your spouse's situation while he or she speaks.
5. Don't finish your spouse's sentences.
6. Don't interrupt.
7. When your spouse is speaking, refrain from looking at your watch.
8. During these conversations, let the phone ring or let the machine take your calls.
9. Most importantly, no matter how tired you are—and if you have kids you're chronically tired—try your best not to fall asleep when your spouse is speaking.

Looking for the Mommy love

A person who is "looking for the Mommy love" is hungry for approval from the outside world. It could be from a boss, a colleague or society at large.

For so many people who are straddling career, parenthood and marriage, looking for the Mommy love can be a sorry distraction. When we're seeking so much approval from the outside world—be it status, a title or a high income—it can backfire on us. That's because when we're searching for the Mommy love, we're willing to spend a lot of time and energy away from the nuclear family to fill ourselves up elsewhere.

Looking for the Mommy love can cause serious problems. The most critical is that it can keep us too preoccupied to give our children the love and attention they need and so rightly deserve. I have witnessed children virtually ignored while being paid off with toys and other material things. These hungry kids likely will suffer the same pattern when they grow up; they are destined to search for the Mommy love.

Searching for outside approval is also hazardous because it can keep us too preoccupied to adequately tend to our spouses.

My husband used to say to me, "I wish you'd think of me," but I was so busy I barely understood what his humble request meant. Now I regret not thinking of him when I often chose work over him or kept myself so busy with projects that I was too worn out to think of him, to check in with him at the end of the day, to give him my support.

It's a question of prioritizing our emotional energies. Think output, input. Try to keep your input to your family significantly higher than your output to the world at large, be it work or social obligations.

If your output greatly surpasses your input, then you may be searching for the Mommy love. To cure yourself of seeking outside approval:

1. Decide to care more about what you think of yourself than what anyone else does.
2. Decide not to be swayed by praise or criticism.

Once you challenge your thinking, you'll be able to slow your frenetic pace, your sprint for the Mommy love. Before long you won't even be tempted to run that race, the one that tethered your emotional energies and left you empty-handed when it came to the most important people in your life: your loved ones.

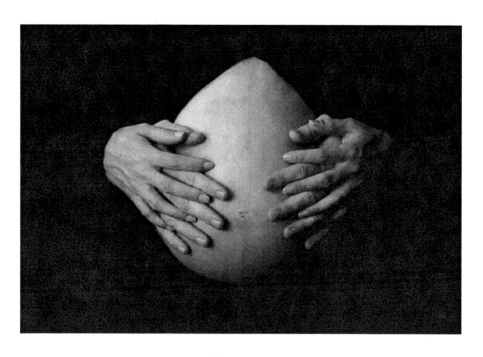

Chapter 4

Plan for chaos

છ

Taxing transitions: zero to one

Expect the first year of a baby's life to make your orbit spin out of control. People who tell you any different are bald-faced liars.

Yes, babies are adorable and, yes, babies smell like heaven. God made them that way so we could endure them. But sleep deprivation makes rookie parents bone tired and the constant worry about keeping their little baby safe and well takes a toll.

And even if you're veteran parents, each time there's a newborn on the scene, expect that first year to be merciless.

Couples, out of sheer exhaustion, can go at each other like pit bulls if they don't restrain themselves. It's hard to fight fair when you feel as though you've been sleepwalking for weeks on end.

Of course, there is one comforting thought to cling to: That first year will be fleeting. When I hear people debating endlessly about having a second child, writing pros and cons every other day, I always think the same thing. Yes, it will be hard that first year, but after that a baby will settle into the orbit.

I learned two things from our hardship. 1) Get as much support as you can. 2) If at all possible, don't travel during the baby's first year.

I took my 2-month-old baby to see my family in Southern California, and it was an exhausting mistake. It was also a travel nightmare, because newborns come with a lot of accessories.

And a lot of demands.

When my baby boy was born, we had quite a difficult transition. I liken it to a war zone because my husband and I seemed like zombies in combat. Too often we were harsh with each other; it took every ounce of energy to be civil.

But before long our baby no longer seemed like a jet-lagged foreigner, sleeping the day away. He got with the program, and we all said a few Hail Marys. Even that member of our family who calls himself a recovering Catholic.

So when you're in a dither, when you're at the brink of madness, remember the countdown. A year is just a fleeting 365 days.

Until then, remember to notice how adorable your baby is and how he smells like heaven.

Build a hut for new parents

There is no better present you can give new bleary-eyed, sleep-deprived parents than a hut.

To understand the concept of the hut, consider the African tradition of bringing up baby. Villagers would build a hut for a mother and her newborn so they could stay put for several months with nothing on their agenda but to bond and rest. They would be pampered by the villagers, who nourished them with meals and gifts.

The modern version of the hut in our harried American culture is altered a bit. First of all, we include Dad in the hut so he, too, can bond and rest. Secondly, we plan a week to 10 days of intensive pampering, because it's hard for us to pull off several months of tending.

So here's the drill: Draw up a list of families who will agree to be on call for a particular day. Each family then volunteers to check in with the new parents, run any necessary errands and supply them with dinner that evening.

I remember how tired we were when my son was born. Just managing to put food on the table was unmanageable. When dinner-time would creep up, my husband and I would look at each other desperately, argue a little and then order out and wait for some restaurant to come to our rescue. But we didn't really want pizza or Chinese food. What we wanted was COMFORT food, homemade soups and stews and pot roasts and mashed potatoes and gravy. We wanted real food, but neither of us had the energy to cook it.

That's when I realized just how nourishing good friends can be and how they can help new parents with a string of home-cooked meals and a lineup of errand runners. Although these services are available for pay, I think it's sweeter when friends band together and organize a "hut." This kind of support can give couples a jumpstart in their first six months of sleep deprivation where tempers run short. A hut can help them stay loving toward each other, celebrate their newest miracle and keep them focused on the baby when the chores of everyday life are handled by loved ones.

So far I've organized a hut for two friends and have watched on while others have organized huts. The goal is to make it a tradition, by having the hut giftees plan a hut for others down the line. And so it begins, this giving tree.

A hut is a simple thing to organize. Everyone wants to be a part of it because everyone wants to drop in and see the new baby, the tired parents, bid them well and leave them with stews, flowers and toys.

It reminds me of the Irish proverb: "It is in the shelter of each other that people live."

When caffeine doesn't work

I swore off caffeine when I was pregnant and I had a stunning revelation: I had been tired for years but I never knew it.

These days I'm back drinking coffee, revving myself up with caffeine in an attempt to delude myself once again. But after two kids, the wonder drug no longer seems to work.

And I am no longer a spry college student recovering from an all-nighter. I am a middle-aged mother trying to recover from a decade of all-nighters. I've reluctantly accepted the cruel fact that, for moms like me, caffeine has become nothing more than a placebo.

When my son recently had croup, we rushed him to the emergency room at 2 a.m., and then one by one caught his virus. This croup affair exacerbated our family's sleep deprivation.

My husband and I would pick on each other for the damnedest things—lax kitchen duty, poor manners, etc.—and my daughter would plead for us to try to get along. (Little people can be such diplomats.) She was right, of course, but when you're bone tired the high road is often beyond reach.

If I seem like I'm complaining, if you think you can hear a violin playing, you're misunderstanding me. I am simply chronicling the facts. I would never trade my children for a life of rest. We parents sacrifice sleep; it's a fair enough tradeoff for the adventure of children.

And yet we have to face facts and compensate for this sleep deprivation, especially since we no longer can pump ourselves up with caffeine. If we don't try to compensate, marital bliss will suffer. So here's my plan:

1. While it sounds obvious, I endeavor to scale down. With children, we naturally take on more obligations, granted. But every time I'm tempted to say yes to a commitment, I practice saying no.
2. When the kids are napping and I'm the only big person in the house, I order myself to nap as well.
3. Finally, I'm challenging myself to reinterpret time. I'm convinced the best way to measure a day is by how gracefully I move through it rather than by how many items I can cross off my to-do list.

I'm just beginning to learn how to move gracefully through time. And I'm encouraged by my progress, although I'm humble enough to realize it will be a lifetime endeavor.

Sleep is heavenly

As I look out the window at the intermittent rain, I'm reminded of my scant night of sleep.

Before I was married with kids I never thought much about sleep. I could get some whenever I wanted it. I could dream for hours on end without interruption. I could wake up slowly or not at all on the weekends. Sleep was plentiful. It was really a non-issue in my life. But that was before I became a parent. A nocturnal animal.

In my current world sleep is a hot and rare commodity. Priceless. Sleep is coveted, bargained and fought for. It's a prize, a grand celebration and a pillowy extravaganza.

Staying happily married with kids when you're sleep-deprived is tough. When the kids are down and I finally begin to enter dreamland, if my husband starts to snore in my ear I cringe, I grope, I nudge him until he stops. My body aches for sleep. I don't care about him anymore. Survival is key. I need my sleep.

Now I know why sleep deprivation was a form of Nazi torture: It causes temporary insanity. And it certainly can play havoc with a marriage.

A great solution to this problem is letting the other guy sleep. It may seem ridiculous, but a key to staying happily married with kids can be as simple as once in a while letting your lover sleep. Here are some real life examples:

#1 One night I was utterly exhausted and the kids were still romping around the house at 9 p.m. My eyelids felt like weights. My husband took one look at my horizontal position on the floor and said, "Hon, it's OK. You look beat. Go ahead and go to sleep. I'll get the kids' jammies on, brush their teeth, read stories to them and put them down. You just go on and get some sleep." I looked at him with deep appreciation. What a kind and merciful husband I have.

#2 It was the crack of dawn on a winter Sunday morning and our 5-year-old stared at me only an inch from my eyeball and shouted: "What's the plan for today, Mom?" She started pulling the covers off my toes, but I could barely utter a sound as my voice box was not functioning yet. My eyelids were still sealed shut. My husband looked at me and said, "You keep sleeping. I'll make breakfast, start the coffee, deal with the kids. You just relax and sleep some more." This was truly rich. I could dream on while the music of the family began without me.

#3 Our kids had been sick for a few days. It was 2 a.m. and one of the kids was screaming. She had a double ear infection. I was searching like a madwoman all through the medicine cabinet for the children's Tylenol. I could barely keep my eyes open, but my husband was wiped out from the night before. I looked at him for a split second as he lay sleeping. I was hoping for some relief but then said, "You can keep sleeping. I'll take care of the baby tonight. I'll catch up with sleep tomorrow." He looked at me and grinned. He grabbed the pillow and rolled over. He was a happy man.

Just a footnote: Instead of fighting over sleep, challenge yourself to think of it as a gift to give. A stretch of sleep is the most kindhearted gift one spouse can give to the other.

When the orbit gets sick

When the kids get sick marriages take a hit. When our daughter had the Siberian flu she moaned continuously for 12 days and nights. Her fever would not subside regardless of extra strength Tylenol, cool baths, popsicles, wet rags and reddish Jell-O. She started losing weight and was dizzy and delirious throughout the ordeal. We couldn't leave her side for more than ten minutes.

During this time our relationship deteriorated quickly. I looked at my husband not as my mate but as a relief worker. All I remember saying to him throughout the 12 days was "It's your turn." Our marriage was reduced to a tag team relay race with opposing team captains. We forgot we were on the same team. Tag. You're it! were the only words I felt like uttering during the days of Tiffany's flu.

They say if you really want to know someone, travel with him. No, I don't think so. If you really want to know someone, marry him, have kids with him and see how he handles things when the kids are sick for more than five days in a row. Dark aspects of each person surface when faced with absolutely no time for oneself.

Harsh words during these times have damaged our feelings toward each other. Phrases like, "You're so lazy and selfish. Can't you help our daughter more?" Or "Rock her more gently. You're not helping her get well fast enough. What's wrong with you?"

For me, learning how to be kind or even civil toward each other during these times was crucial to staying happily married with kids. When I think of how we cursed and were so nasty to one another during these times I cringe. Yet I know 12 sleepless nights and 11 housebound days could do that to anyone. We have had many sick days since the Siberian flu, and here is a list of tips we've accumulated over the past decade that have helped us stay loving toward each other even when fevers are high and the help is run down.

1. Beg all known relatives and true friends for breaks.
2. Get videos both you and the kids can handle.
3. Use a headset on your cell or land line.
4. Give your spouse short breaks to shower or meditate or pray.
5. Muster the strength to compliment your spouse.
6. Try to be thankful you have a spouse to help you during this time.

Don't book back-to-back

I used to book back-to-back, but then my husband went on strike, arguing he didn't have the social stamina to weather my scheduling.

Husbands and wives, I'm convinced, have different wattage. And while one energy level is not better than another, it's a good idea to know your mate's. My husband, Tim, is 300 volts, while I'm closer to 1000.

Tim likes time to himself and finds too much social hubbub stressful. As for me, I seem to draw energy from others, like the moon reflecting the sun's light. I don't require much alone time and hate to miss an adventure.

All marriages have to compromise on energy output, but this is especially important when you add children to the mix. As one friend so eloquently put it: Children suck the life out of you.

True enough. Children can take a toll on even high-wattage parents. Accompanying your spouse to a party is one thing. Patrolling a toddler at a party is quite another. It will make you rethink the merit of social outings altogether, particularly when porcelain and fine linen are involved.

I no longer see any point in scheduling back-to-back, two parties and a book club meeting in one day, or a string of dinners out three nights in a row. Even if my husband didn't go on strike, my kids couldn't possibly behave for three hours in a row. It's a statistical impossibility.

I remember one day I was so excited to take my son to a Halloween party hosted by two of his preschool buddies. We had RSVP-ed and even had a ready supply of candy to pass out. But that day I was running late, and by the time I picked my son up, I realized we'd have 35 minutes to spend at the party before we'd have to pack it up for the next event, a Halloween dinner party at our house.

I reluctantly picked up my cell and called one of the preschool moms, explaining that our day had gotten away from us and we'd have to pass on the party.

I looked in the back of the car at Buzz Lightyear in his car seat and I felt disappointed and relieved all in one breath. I knew I didn't have the energy to herd a wired kid from one party to the next. We all have our limits, and happily mine have humbled me into being a realistic planner. I scored "sensitivity" points with husband on this one. He appreciates that I've attempted to slow the family's pace.

One dinner out a week is plenty. One party a weekend is our maximum capacity. I've learned to keep a lean schedule and, more importantly, factor in flexibility.

Going up the down escalator

Often cleaning the house feels like an escalator ride in the wrong direction. Each moment you pick up, straighten, scrub, wipe, swipe, sweep, fold and arrange, it seems like the little people in your house follow you around with the sole intention of undoing all your doings.

And, well, that's what little people do.

When my frustration began to reach new heights a few years ago, I knew it was time to create a system. I simply thought we all have to take part in cleaning. Now our 5-year-old and 9-year-old have a list of chores as long as the list my husband and I tackle. I no longer fold all of the kids' clothes. Some mothers gawk at this and say, "A small child can't keep their laundry in order."

But I witness it on a regular basis.

Our 9-year-old sorts a good chunk of laundry each week. Sorting is a good math activity, right? She separates her sister's clothes from any parent clothes and puts her own away in her dresser. Our 5-year-old also folds her own clothes, and if need be, we help her or we ask the 12-year-old neighbor to help her for two or three dollars a week. My husband and I put away our own clothes, and sanity has been restored. Laundry madness no longer rules this castle.

When it comes to other chores such as washing dishes and sweeping, we have a chart to follow and the kids have daily and weekly chores. And, yes, they do get perks if they complete their work. But their allowance, play dates and prizes are worth it because Mom and Dad are no longer the only employees in the house. Now we are all chipping in to help the household stay in some semblance of order. The kids don't give us any back talk and, in fact, they seem happier as insiders, part of the team.

When parents feel overwhelmed with shopping, cooking, cleaning and organizing the laundry for four or more, something has to give, and better the kids than the sanity of a parent.

Morning drive: How to tame the madness

Before we had kids we always had to rush to get ready for work or school, scurrying to get ourselves showered, dressed, fed and ready to walk out the door. But being married with kids gives new meaning to the word "rush." Getting three or four people out of the house all at the same time, all in the same state of readiness, takes planning. It takes stamina. It takes courage.

The old saying "If you fail to plan, you plan to fail" really does apply here. Without strategic maneuvering, the mornings can be so stressful that by 7 a.m. my husband and I start barking at each other. It isn't pretty. Even our dog will hide from us.

So we begin the process the night before. Otherwise we sink.

I take care of my needs in advance. I shower, I pick out my clothes and I put all of the things I need for work in the car. My husband picks out his clothes and lays them out on his dresser. He stashes his keys and wallet in a safe place, a place the kids can't find. We also get the kids to pick out their clothes. Otherwise we end up arguing with them at 7 a.m. about why it's not OK to wear a sleeveless summer dress when its freezing outside and how the Winnie The Pooh underwear is not available because it's in the dirty laundry pile.

We get the kids to start packing the nonperishables in their lunch boxes the night before to prepare for the morning madness we call "rush it up." I create a special place for my husband to put his work stuff so we don't have the mad search for his papers at 6 a.m. He even picks his shoes out the night before. Silly? We think not. With small kids the teeth-brushing and hair-combing battles alone can cause a pre-dawn nervous breakdown.

Despite our great planning, we still falter. One morning I thought I had it down. Husband fed and gone, kids in the car, teeth brushed, hair combed, car seats fastened. I began driving down the road feeling in control when I noticed a plate of cookies flying across the street and I thought, "What idiot throws a plate of cookies out a window?" And then I realized I am that idiot. It's my plate of cookies flying down the street, the one I set on top of the car while loading kids and accessories.

Then I looked down and I noticed my shirt was inside out. One of the pitfalls of dressing three people at once. At least the kids were safe and my keys were in the ignition.

Planning won't necessarily make mornings seamless, but it's certain to do one thing: keep couples from barking at each other at sunrise.

The family car ride—
survival is key

We jokingly refer to our 3-year-old as the little Emperor. But when our family is taking a trip in the car and our nerves are shot, the royal highness is never so privileged.

"Give him whatever the hell he wants," my husband bellowed on a recent trip after a wrong turn put us in a bad neighborhood in Oakland. A thick early morning haze made the streets look smoky.

My son got the toy he wanted and we scored a moment of calm to navigate ourselves back to the freeway.

We were on a 9-hour odyssey to San Diego from Santa Rosa and things weren't looking pretty. We weren't even outside the Bay Area and we were already starting to lose it.

The family car ride, as a rule, requires the patience of a saint. Considering that we parents are mere mortals and patience is often an insurmountable goal, we need a strategy to cohabitate with children in a moving vehicle.

If you don't have a strategy, you're likely to make bonehead moves like the one I made at a Quik-Mart.

The little Emperor wanted a toy, and after threatening an all out tantrum, I bought it for him. I was hoping to get 30 minutes of uninterrupted quiet.

But when I got back to the car and informed my husband of my purchase, he took one look at me and thought I'd gone mad. I had unwittingly bought a dart gun with projectile bullets, endangering the safety of our driver.

Our son wasn't about to give up his prize and all we could do was laugh as we pooled our creative talents to devise a plan to snatch the misfit toy from him.

In the end we survived the marathon car ride, barely, bonehead moves and all. We congratulated ourselves on some smart tactics and vowed to learn from the not-so-smart ones.

Here are some pointers for parents like us who are prone to surges of impatience when trapped in a car with yapping children.

1. Get an early start, preferably at 4 a.m. when a moving car can lull kids back to sleep for a few hours. You may be tired when you arrive, but you'll be less exhausted from tussling with the kids. Best of all, the trip seems shorter for everyone, including the driver.

2. Take a portable television/VCR and rig it up in the back seat with two sets of headphones for the kids. Pack up all their favorite movies and let them be media-hyped TV junkies for a day. You don't have to be politically correct at all times.

3. Create a wet bar in the car, non-alcoholic of course, with plenty of drinks and snacks on hand.

4. Pack quiet toys and books. Steer clear of toys that honk and beep, ones that could compromise the safety and well-being of the driver, not to mention his or her sanity.

Prepare to compromise. Remember your kid(s) are trapped in the back of a car for hours on end, and that's asking a lot. Keep in mind the little Emperor isn't used to adverse conditions. On the contrary, he's used to being pampered.

The bewitching hour

Peg's story

It's eerie the way it happens every night, as if the rising moon outside were responsible for the howling children inside.

At 5 p.m., the official end of our work day, children are tired. And when children are exhausted you can hardly reason with them, a relative once told me. She was right. Fatigue makes consequences null and void. Likewise, threats and bribes.

Parents, many beginning their second shift at home, are also tired and they're operating without the traditional parenting tools to rein in children.

After much trial and error (mostly error), we've discovered that the best way to deal with unruly children at this hour is play with them full throttle. We simply delay dinner or have one spouse man the kitchen while the other mans the children.

Whether it's Play Doh, Legos or a computer game, kids will be able to hold it together better if they have a parent's full attention. So during the bewitching hour, we no longer answer our phone. We no longer lollygag with the neighbors. We don't choose Steak au Poivre over the children. Instead we romp with them. We surprise the kids (and ourselves) by giving them more attention than they expect, more than we think we can muster.

Once they get their fill of attention, kids typically will walk away and give you a moment. But rest assured, if you don't make yourself 100 percent available during the bewitching hour, your children will come back to haunt you.

Leslie's story

Homework is done. Papers fall into backpacks. The phone rings. The doorbell sounds like a siren. The water's boiling for pasta. The oven sets off the smoke alarm. I drop noodles into hot water. I burn the French bread. The kids cry in hunger. My husband walks in and says "Hi, what's cookin?" The dog sighs as he shadows my every move hoping for burnt bread crumbs. My back aches behind the right shoulder blade and I groan.

The family rhythm beats fast and furious. John Steinbeck refers to "The music of the family" in his novel "The Pearl." He describes the sound of the mother as she pounds corn cakes, the baby as he cries and the father as he drags in his fish catch of the day.

There is a time of day when the music roars through every room in this house. I feel like I'm conducting an orchestra with 100 instruments all playing at full capacity. My husband and I team up as conductors who try to set the band in perfect harmony. We try to pull the players together every evening for a harmonious concert. If we're in harmony the other players chime in.

It's time to make magic happen. When the energy of tired kids, tired mom, tired dad and hunger converge in on you at once you have probably entered what we call the bewitching hour. In our house this occurs between 5 and 7 p.m. It's as if someone casts a spell on our family, which simply transforms each of us in to ill-tempered witches and wizards desperate for a potion to end this spell.

My husband and I have found some secret potions that help us remain loving towards each other and the kids during the bewitching hour.

We have 10 ingredients for a magical spell to cast upon these hours.

1. Never answer the phone during the spell.
2. Ignore the doorbell during this time.
3. Spend ten minutes talking to your spouse when you greet each other. Share a glass of something. Kiss before snapping.
4. Kiss each kid twice.
5. Take a deep breath and remember these hours go quickly
6. Plan dinner earlier in the day.
7. Request that everyone help cook and set the table.
8. Create quick meals and plop an appetizer on the table. Appease the hunger fast.
9. Light a candle and say a prayer of any kind.
10. Try to feel appreciative.

Make magic happen. And, *voilá*, dinner is served.

When we yell at the kids

Kids can change you in many ways, mostly in positive ways. One becomes less selfish, more concerned with others, a better negotiator. But kids also can push our limits to the point of no return. A seemingly healthy person can start yelling in a way one never thought possible.

The scary moment arrives when you see your spouse losing it and you wonder, why is he yelling like a madman? The last time my husband did this his voice pierced through the house like a siren and my eardrums began to pound. I felt like I was being yelled at even though the yelling was directed at the kids. The sound waves bounced off all walls and boomeranged back at me.

Beware: This type of behavior can cause one to lose interest in one's spouse.

My husband also has told me that when I scream across the living room for the kids to stop fighting it's a real turn-off for him; he does not find me at all attractive when I'm screaming. Funny. I thought I always looked good even when I was yelling. What to do?

Here's our solution that has helped us remain sane during those moments when we begin yelling. We slow down, count to ten, and go right over to the kid in question and talk to him or her directly in a low pitched voice. We don't yell across the house anymore. This diffuses most of the tension and saves our eardrums too. If necessary we leave the room and hide out in the backyard.

Once when our baby cried for three hours in a row I began to fall apart. I called a nurse at a local hospital who suggested something wise. Here's what she said: "Put the baby in her crib. And as long as the baby is safe, step outside and count to 50 before stepping back in the house." Even though our kids are now seven and eleven, I apply this advice often. Fresh air can do wonders when the air is too hot inside the casa.

Chapter 5

Negotiations

Marriage is one long, unwieldy negotiation

Keep closing the deal

☙

Waves

The best love comes in waves.

I've fallen in love with my husband countless times, and it always happens the same way. A wave of humor. A wave of kindness. A wave of playfulness. Somehow he wins me over, even after a contentious point, counterpoint.

It can be simple. Like the time he helped my son open his birthday present, a baseball mitt and ball, and asked "Where's his million dollar contract?"

Or the time he followed me around the kitchen, his face in mine, telling me that despite our fierce debate, "You can still kiss me, you know."

Or when I was driving my car, following him in his, and another car merged between us, he pulled off the road to make sure I didn't lose my way.

These sweet gestures always manage to calm any harsh winds between us and, frankly, a marriage with kids is turbulent at best. Of course the way we used to fight created even more bluster. We used to distance ourselves routinely during a fight and for hours after, a sorry side effect of our frustration.

What's worse, our arguments had a tendency to race from one topic to the next, complicating things. In one argument, household duties, money worries and independence versus responsibility collected, amassing in a dark cloud.

Discouraged, I asked for advice from a friend who had struggled with her marriage, and she had this answer: stay engaged. She said you can't expect much movement or change to occur if either of you disengages from the relationship.

To fight smart, both stay engaged to resolve the problems, no matter how hot the argument, she said.

It makes sense. If someone has one foot in the relationship and one foot out, the argument becomes a different argument altogether. The stakes are higher, and each spouse feels more vulnerable.

Add kids to the mix and you begin to feel even more unsteady. That's because when you're in combat with your spouse, children escalate the tension. They see that you're preoccupied and vie for your attention. A truce, when possible, is a wise parenting policy.

My friend said it's not hard to stay engaged if you're mindful of your spouse's best nature, even when you're tempted to roar at each other.

I think this goes down as the best advice I've ever received. Because when you marry someone, you make a commitment. And that commitment should be to be mindful of your spouse's best nature for a lifetime.

I went home and vowed never to distance myself again. In fact, I have come full circle. These days when we're in the middle of a heated debate, I joke to my husband that we should make love and follow my friend's advice to stay engaged.

Separate but Equal

There is no way a relationship can work unless both parties are equal.

I have seen it countless times, the slow, cancerous death of a relationship when one spouse—either overtly or covertly—bullies the other.

Bullies, for the record, come in two breeds. They are either belligerent or self-righteous. If they're belligerent, they tend to honk off at their mate in public. If they're self-righteous, they prefer the subtle, passive-aggressive posture: humiliation by slights.

If you think for one minute that things are going well because you've gotten your way for a decade or so, think again. At some point the relationship will falter.

At my house we have achieved a balance of power; we're definitely on equal footing. I won't let him get away with anything and he won't let me either. I'm happy about this because a marriage of equals shows our children that the best union is that of two strong wills.

Here's how I see it. Speaking out is a muscle that should be exercised each and every time someone's out of line. Before long you get so comfortable speaking your mind, you can speak it for hours on end.

Couples need to have a balance of power, and if they don't, they should keep working toward this. In the end everybody wants a strong, no-nonsense spouse. Someone who can stand up to a fast-talking car salesman or a snippety teen-ager.

In the end, what we long for is an equal.

Red alert

The most alarming thing about a red alert is that it comes without a siren. Figuring why a marriage is going south will keep you scratching your head for days, if not decades.

It helps to be aware of troublesome signs.

The most troubling is when you begin to recast the players in your life, casting out your spouse. You may begin to develop a roving eye, searching for someone who would make the ideal spouse. Perhaps you even have a lover on the side, keeping your marriage hanging by a thread. Or it could be as simple as spending too much time thinking about your old college lost love whom you could have/should have married.

If you're tempted to construct a life without your spouse, consider yourself in crisis. No matter how innocuous it may seem, it should warn you that your marriage is seriously off track.

A woman once told me she had a terrible crush on a man and, given all of her marital troubles, her life may take a different path. She didn't mention a path with a third party. She didn't have to.

Another woman, who was having a terrible time taming her workaholic husband, said she solved the problem. She simply began taking an anti-depressant and so she wasn't sad when he was preoccupied.

Both of these women were in crisis. A siren should have been blaring but the danger lurked below the surface as elusive as a whisper.

I'm not sure if either of these women compounded the crisis by bandying around the D-word (divorce) in heated arguments. Talk of divorce to retaliate can escalate tensions and set this fantasy life in motion. It provokes both parties to secretly plan a life without the other, just in case.

If this should ever happen to you, shake some sense into yourself and get some help. Remember your vow, for better, for worse, for rainy day heartache.

Other telltale signs include:

> When you don't want to hear about your spouse's day.
> When you no longer care about what's going on at your spouse's work.
> When you always put the kids first.
> When you no longer feel attracted to your spouse.
> When you no longer sleep together.
> Or when sex becomes less and less frequent, once every six months . . . wake-up call.

Don't go to bed mad

A woman I knew who'd been married with kids for a while gave me this sage advice when I got married: "Never go to bed angry and sleep in the same bed even after fighting." Sure, I thought, that sounds simple enough.

On my wedding day I assumed I'd always want to sleep in the same bed as my husband, regardless of any marital spat we might have.

When we had our first big fight my instinct was to completely avoid this man. Sleeping with the enemy was unthinkable. I would go lie on the couch and curl up in a fetal position. I would bury my face deep in a pillow and only emerge for air. When he'd come after me with his pleas for forgiveness I couldn't fathom re-establishing eye contact. I felt like I could never forgive him. Why should I? He was wrong. Or was he?

As the night grew darker and, as dawn approached, I simmered, I stewed, I cried. I forgot how the argument began, but I was still fuming. He came toward the couch again and stood there begging me to come to bed. But I was paralyzed by my own negativity. It was as if forces beyond my control wouldn't let me budge or even look at him. Then he said in a soft voice, "Remember the advice we got? Never go to bed mad, make up before morning, sleep in the same bed. Come on honey, you know neither of us will get any rest until you come to bed."

Something clicked for me just then and I was able to open my eyes and stare at him standing there half-naked, looking so vulnerable and kind. I pulled myself out of the hell of being angry and hugged him. I wrapped my arms around him and walked with him down the hall back to our bed. We kissed and went to sleep; the fight officially ended.

With children surrounding us now we can't always argue freely, and it's tough to keep all disagreements PG-13. The only time we could set up our angry camps were when the kids were asleep.

But these days, when one of us shuts down emotionally and goes straight to the couch mad, the other will come to the couch and stand in some ridiculous posture wearing nothing but slippers. One of us will always say, "Hey, we can't go to bed angry, let's resolve it and go back to bed." Sometimes sleeping with the enemy creates a lifelong comrade.

The Perry Mason of love

There's plenty of courtroom drama at my house, although all the cases involve a misdemeanor: the elusive double standard.

My husband calls me "The Perry Mason of Love" because I can be a relentless interrogator when I sense a hint of injustice.

Money is a hot issue in most marriages, but I think it's even more pronounced in ours because our view of money is at two ends of a spectrum. My husband sees money as a saving device, while I see it as a spending device.

I noticed a double standard when my husband attempted to make me the designated small-scale spender due to my enthusiastic spending philosophy.

Here's one good example. He wanted me to buy the budget toys for the kids' holiday gifts while he focused on the expensive ones. I was taken aback. I mean, how fun is that?

To be fair, I don't think it was an attempt to usurp my power as an equal. My husband simply loves to shop for expensive newfangled, electronic kid gadgets that require hordes of batteries, extension cords, nuts and bolts, and manuals that take hours to decipher.

While I'm not particularly mechanically minded, I love buying hot-shot toys, too, so I argued the point. He countered that it was more sensible for him to be the big budget toy spender because he's far more prudent than I am. He reminded me of my financial plan: spend freely, earn more later.

I was amused but proceeded to argue. Talking to him didn't help. The only thing that changed the situation was when I began to track his toy spending. It turns out he is just as irresponsible as I am when it comes to buying irresistible, expensive toys; that man has just as many cost overruns.

Before long, he stopped trying to control who bought what.

It's important to get a relationship that's off-kilter back in balance, because the relationship is a model for kids. We need to teach children that relationships are on an equal playing field. Otherwise we run the risk of raising children to think marriage is a union in which one dominates or will be dominated.

The first time my husband called me the Perry Mason of Love, I had a good laugh. But after the laugh subsided, I realized every couple actually needs a designated Perry Mason to question double standards.

After all, the best relationships are fair, and to that end, you may have to cross examine your spouse from time to time.

10 p.m. curfew on the money blues

A friend once said the best trouble to have is money troubles because the situation can change at any moment. Health problems and heartaches don't have such swift remedies.

And yet worry is the all-American pastime for many families like mine who count the unpaid bills at the end of the month and rush to shift money from one account to another.

A ban on late-night worrying is a smart policy because when we grow weary, worry can spin out of control and flash into blame. Before you know it you're fighting with your spouse over something purchased 10 years ago that has absolutely no bearing on the issue at hand.

We've had far too many midnight misguided quarrels, so these days I only argue 9 to 5.

No kidding.

I recently flat-out canceled an argument one night because my husband and I were simply too tired to take it on. I just called the whole thing off, telling my husband he'd have to argue with himself because I was going to sleep. I told him I'd be happy to resume the argument the next morning after we were well rested.

He wasn't amused and tried to tease me back into the fray. I pretended to snore and that was that.

Worry and the kind of arguing it provokes is frustrating. More importantly, it's off point.

You see, in the middle of the night it's hard to keep perspective on money troubles. It's hard to see them for what they are: the best troubles to have.

Debriefing your spouse

The President may need daily cabinet meetings to make decisions for national security, but being married with kids can require hourly briefings just to keep track of everyone's whereabouts.

Just the other day we were trying to figure out how to get one kid to a Girl Scout meeting, the other to a basketball practice, one spouse to a meeting and the other to a yoga class.

Aside from logistics, we had to plan how to divvy up duties. Who would help our older daughter with a homework project due the next day? Who would help our little one with her reading log?

After years of chaotic, free-for-all haggling with kids endeavoring to decide the day, we concluded democracy is not our politics of choice. If it's a matter of rule or be ruled, we prefer to reign.

So we steal away from the kids and search out a private spot. The backyard. The garage. We've even resorted to the bathroom.

Once secluded, we become CEOs of sorts, negotiating, strategizing, compromising. We route the kids, delegate homework duties and discuss what's on the docket for tomorrow.

We realize that if we don't act quickly, our kids will try to take matters into their own hands. For example, one morning our older daughter was on the phone making plans with two friends to bike at the park and maybe see a movie later. Our younger daughter had called her seven-year-old buddy and began begging for a play date at another park.

Debriefing each other keeps the day from being up for grabs.

I used to expect my husband to read my mind, to know who, what, where, when and why. But those days are over. I've come to realize that even telepathy couldn't possibly make him privy to everyone's daily planner.

Debriefing each other has become as natural as saying "bye" each time we part. It's as if we're hardwired with internal magnets that pull us together to confer constantly. Our pow-wows also provide us with a continuous type of "check in" time where we see how the other person's day is going and how the other is feeling.

At times my husband's the lighthouse and I'm the ship searching for his light to guide me, and at other times he's the ship searching for my light. Our conversations keep us both afloat in this sea of parenthood. And our efforts to connect create a loving, caring tenderness on which we both thrive.

Chapter 6

Stay close to your spirit

Find ways to nurture yourself

☙

Find a "sanctuary" (spa) with day care

As my body melts into the hot walls, I stare with no particular focus at the steam rising to fill my pores with wet warmth.

I have an entire hour of not hurrying in front of me. I feel hopeful. I have no worries right this second. I breathe in deeply, and the smell of eucalyptus fills my lungs. I exhale and realize this is the first deep breath I have had all week.

Droplets of steam cover me now. I decide to enter the hot tub slowly, anticipating the warmth of streaming jets. I position my body at an angle so that the force of gushing water hits my upper back and hip where I hurt most. My body has severely shifted since having two kids, and the jets soothe my aches. Bubbles surround me and I smile.

My kids are booked in the day care on the premises for another 39 minutes. I close my eyes and relish the heat as I ponder my teaching strategies, errands to run and what my family will eat tonight. I try to shut down my mind. I say to myself. "You're doing your best. It's OK if you don't get it all done today."

My bones feel warm. I peek at the dry sauna room but opt for a long shower instead. I let the hot water run down my spine. I have that extra five minutes needed to shave without nicking my skin. No one is yelling, "Mom, get out of the shower!" or "Honey, can't you speed it up? I've got to leave the house now." Ahhhhhh. The luxury of a lingering shower. Decadence.

I get dressed without rushing through the process. I can almost smell and taste the silence. I actually hear my own voice in my head. A rarity at home. I look in the mirror as I put on my rouge and I feel clean, organized and as if my body has been revived from a minor battle.

I approach the day-care room filled with appreciation. I look forward to spending time with the kids. I feel love for my husband because he encouraged me to join this place even though it's a squeeze for us financially. But I've come to the conclusion that this is a sanctuary I can't afford to do without. Even if it means cutting back elsewhere to balance our budget, having a place like this with day care available seven days a week is essential for my well being. And my well being is a smart health plan for my family.

Cause if Mamma ain't happy, ain't nobody happy.

The flame dancing within

When you're married with kids there's a prevailing reason to keep close to your spirit: It's to make sure you appreciate your children, these little flower buds unfurling each and every day. It's to make sure you don't get caught up in the mundane and miss the moment . . . the first step, the first word, the first swim meet, the first dance. Children grow up in the blink of an eye, and the only thing that can keep you from blinking is spirituality.

By the same token you want to live in the moment with your spouse, to keep that sweet connection each and every day. And, to be frank, living in a loud house with kids romping around can be most unromantic.

So what you need is a few props: incense, fragrant cut flowers and candles, to name a few. But if I had to pick one prop to romance my husband, it would be candles every time. Candles soften a setting and transform a room.

I've actually heard that candles and their sweet, soft light can turn down the wattage in children and keep them mild-mannered. Although I don't believe in subliminal communication on a regular basis, I make an exception when it comes to candles. I keep a ready supply within reach when I want to have a glass of wine with my husband before dinner.

We also have plenty of candles lit during dinner, and it somehow makes the whole meal sweeter, a lingering affair rather than a fast-food stop.

A candle, for me, best embodies the spirit, a flame dancing within. It is the best part of us, the part that tells the truth, the part that is rock-solid certain, the part that tells people off when we need to, the part that keeps us close to God in whatever incarnation, the part that keeps us uplifted.

When I'm alone I like to pray in the company of candles. I pray big pervasive, all-important prayers for humanity, for world peace, for an end to hunger, for a cure for cancer. But I also pray a humble prayer for myself. I pray that I can keep close to my spirit, the best part of me, my flame dancing within.

Create a spiritual corner

As a wife, mother and educator, I've found it essential to actually create a spiritual corner in my own home where I pray, meditate and reflect quietly.

A spiritual corner can be religious in nature or simply relaxing. It can be an altar in your living room, a corner of candles near your bathtub, a window sill with special flowers and a rosary, or a comfy chair with special books nearby.

When my husband underwent surgery during the summer of 2000, I was in the waiting room when the nurse mentioned that there was a meditation room available. I thought this rather avant-garde for a huge hospital chain, but I entered. The lights were low, a water fountain trickled, there were mats and purple pillows on the floor and a Tiffany lamp on a low table. There was an array of reading material: The Bible, The Jewish Book of Wisdom, the Koran and a book of Buddhist teachings. A spiritual corner for all faiths. How wise.

At home no one is undergoing surgery, but life with children often can make you feel as though you're living in an intensive-care unit with a staff of two. A spiritual corner provides a place for either spouse to go and meditate, or just plain pray to make it to the kids' bedtime with some composure. This way you can crack a smile at your spouse before you both fall asleep in a huddle.

You could create a spiritual corner, even if it's a small space. Even if no one else realizes that it's Mom or Dad's special place to think, to re-energize.

My husband and I often get interrupted by the kids when we're in our spiritual corner, but even an interrupted spiritual infusion rejuvenates the spirit.

Make gratefulness your mantra

Some days my mind feels like a pinball machine, with one stressful thought ricocheting off another.

I was en route to drop my son off to his day care when I began to fret. What if I'm late for work? What if I'm late for my interview? What if I can't get the information I need today? What if I'm late with my story?

And so on.

Luckily, my toddler babbled, distracting me from my stressful spiral of worries. I babbled back at him and then decided, SO WHAT? So what if I'm late for work? So what if I miss my interview? So what if I don't get the information I need? So what if I'm late with my story? After all, I can always troubleshoot a solution.

I had to laugh at myself and so many of us crazed parents who nickel and dime ourselves—five minutes here, 10 minutes there—out of life with worthless worry.

That day was when I determined to become a reformed hurrier. I resolved to quiet my noisy thoughts and replenish my mind with grateful thoughts every time I begin a spate of wayward worrying.

And so it began, this plan to make gratefulness my mantra.

My husband is pleased with my effort because worrying makes for an unfocused mate, one who is prone to burn the rice or forget to turn off the sprinkler. A rash of these annoying instances can fester and cause major blowouts, with one of us chiding the other one (that would be me) for not paying attention to life.

Relentless hurry can also lead to a slew of speeding tickets, yet another bone of contention in our marriage. Hurrying hasn't been good for my driving record.

Of course, hurrying has made for some great stories. My husband loves the one where I outsmarted a cop by exiting the highway, entering a used-car lot and ducking down. The copper followed me off the exit but he couldn't find me among the used cars.

Naturally, that was before I had kids and I hurried just for sport. Today, with kids, hurrying is a habit that's hard to shake. There's so much in our lives to rush to and rush from.

But, in the end, I know hurrying is a pathetic waste of time.

When I shut down the worry and let gratefulness stream through my senses, I feel relaxed, focused and happy. I thank God for my family, my soul mate husband, my good-hearted daughter and my spirited son.

And I'm grateful I'm a reformed hurrier. In fact, I would stand up and boast about it at any 12-step program, that is, if there were such a program as Hurrier's Anonymous.

One morning without rushing up

Peg's story

One lazy Sunday I woke up to some strange bedfellows: a black lab, a toddler and a pre-teen had jumped in with me. They decided it would be fun to read in bed, so we set up camp, huddling around a book and nibbling on Cheerios from the box.

Outside rain tap danced on the patio.

I was supposed to go to a meeting which would have called a halt to the whole affair, this impromptu breakfast-in-bed, and I didn't have the heart. I skipped the meeting and pretended my bed was an island, a refuge from the fast-paced world of hurry.

I made a game of it, hoping to keep the kids and dog cozy in bed for as long as the book would hold their attention. We actually stayed in bed for an hour and a half, and I never ventured out all day.

This slow-moving day reminded me of our vacation in Kauai a few years ago and how my dear husband boasted he was proud to be an underachiever on the trip.

He said he was happy sipping umbrella drinks and playing with the kids by the pool at the hotel, never venturing off the premises.

I've found that weekends are a prime time for me to be an underachiever. The slow-paced days give me a chance to play with my kids, as well as spend time with my husband. I never realized how nourishing it is to do nothing but bask in my family.

These days I block out as much unhurried time as I can spare on the weekends. At least one morning without rushing up.

Leslie's story

When I was eight years old I remember telling my Grandma that I wished to God that time would speed up. I told her I wanted to be all grown up and the boss of me. She laughed and said. "Honey, the older you get, the faster time goes. Before you know it you'll be wishing you could slow time down." I said, "I don't think so, Grandma."

Now I experience daily what Grandma talked about. Since getting married and having kids it's as if each day blends in to the next quicker than water rushes down Niagara Falls. Nonstop and vigorous.

Today, I relish not rushing. For me, staying happily married with kids hinges on finding ways to slow down time. I endeavor to create what I call "slow time." I am learning to be the master of our family time. I have become a time manager who tries to make time stop and take notice of our love for each other. Taming time is no easy feat when kids run wild with energy, but I try.

On Sundays we race nowhere. Kids snooze past 8 a.m. Slow-moving children eat Cheerios and watch cartoons. My husband and I cling to the bed for as long as possible. Sometimes we make love or dip in the hot tub. Coffee brews. We sit and talk.

The girls join us in making eggs and waffles. The smell of bacon fills the air. We actually eat breakfast together. No one gets dressed till way past 10 a.m. It's our day to not rush up.

Find wise advice

My wise woman has kind, green eyes and hair streaked with gray.

In her house, she always has tea brewing in a pot on her stove, fresh-cut flowers on her counter and cats loafing on the sofa, snoozing to the drumming of African music.

I see her as a medicine woman, albeit a New Age medicine woman.

A massage therapist, she can tell people all about their muscles, bones and joints. As a wise soul, she also knows about people's deep tissue, their emotional aches and pains.

I am eternally grateful to my wise woman because her spiritual guidance helped my marriage.

At the time, my mother-in-law was living with us and she lost her job one day unexpectedly. This forced me to continue working full time when I wanted to cut back to spend more time with the baby. My wise woman told me that God put my mother-in-law in my path for a reason. I was supposed to learn a lesson about setting my course rather than letting circumstances dictate my life. Soon my husband and I came up with a plan to live on our own within six months' time. We assured my mother-in-law that we would help her make a smooth transition elsewhere, as well as help her find a job. We held up our end of the bargain and, within six months, my mother-in-law moved into an apartment. The new arrangement significantly improved our relationship as a couple. Wisdom can keep married couples united. Thanks to my wise woman I learned how to set my course, as well as sail with ease. She helped me put my spirituality into my day-to-day living.

Finding some measure of spirituality on a day-to-day basis is crucial because living in a house with a spouse, children, and sometimes a few guests is anything but serene.

I have learned a great deal from my wise woman and her patient ways, her inspiring words and her philosophical view of everyday living. I ask her advice every so often, and she always has time for me because wise women are never in a hurry.

I love to talk with her because she lives deeper than most; life, for her, comes in more brilliant hues. She's always noticing things, a plant in bloom, a song's lyrics. And she's always making brilliant discoveries from stories or commentaries she has heard. Like the time she said people prefer to live a life without pain, but souls deep within people like to grow so people just have to put up with some pain now and again.

Everybody needs a wise woman, a person who can inspire them to put some semblance of spirituality into their day-to-day regimen. Find one.

A medical scare

A few years ago at an educator's conference I was seeking career advice and a wise man looked at me and said, "Your career seems to be going well, but don't undervalue your husband or family." I thought, yeah, yeah, yeah, what's he babbling about? I came here for career advice and I care plenty about my husband and family.

Two weeks after my return from the conference I found myself in a hospital with my husband where he underwent a routine procedure.

During the middle of it the nurse came out to get me. I knew it was odd cause they just don't do that. When I entered the room with the doctor he explained that he detected a tumor and did not know if it was benign or cancerous.

As the words came out of the doctor's mouth, time seemed to be suspended. I wasn't really there at all, but in some horrid nightmare. My life was shaken to the core. All the petty stuff I usually obsessed over meant nothing.

We waited a week until the surgery. During this procedure they would check to see if the tumor was benign and, if so, remove it. If it was cancerous, the doctor said, treatment options would be discussed. During the week prior to the surgery my husband and I, who are Buddhists, chanted sincerely for his health for many hours each day.

I reflected on my love for him and what that wise man mentioned to me at the educator's conference. How much did I value this man and my family? Were my priorities really in check? I changed that week. I realized that wise man was right. I did undervalue my husband.

During his surgery I prayed. We were fortunate. His tumor was actually a benign cyst. But our relationship changed dramatically after this episode. I take nothing for granted. I treasure every day with him and my children. A medical scare changed my perspective on married life with kids. I realized with the core of my life how precious each day truly is. I love my husband on a much deeper level today and I feel joy each day I get to share with him, regardless of the stress we experience as parents.

I love him more now than the day I met him. I never realized how much I treasured his life.

About the Authors

Leslie Kaplan, M.A., teaches English for the Santa Rosa Junior College in Sonoma County, Ca. She also teaches for the Education Department of Sonoma State University. Kaplan got married in 1989 and began having kids in 1990. She's still madly in love with her husband.

Peg Melnik, M.A., is co-author of the "Napa & Sonoma Book," and she is a veteran columnist and new blogger with the New York Time's-owned Press Democrat, the premiere newspaper in Sonoma County. Melnik has been happily married since 1986, and she's an unabashed romantic with two angelic, albeit spirited kids.